T0348403

Fundamentals of Fund Administration: A Guide

Fundamentals of Fund Administration: A Guide

A Complete Guide from Fund Set Up to Settlement and Beyond

David Loader

ELSEVIER

Amsterdam • Boston • Heidelberg • London
New York • Oxford • Paris • San Diego
San Francisco • Singapore • Sydney • Tokyo

Butterworth-Heinemann is an imprint of Elsevier

Butterworth-Heinemann is an imprint of Elsevier
Linacre House, Jordan Hill, Oxford OX2 8DP, UK
30 Corporate Drive, Suite 400, Burlington, MA 01803, USA

First edition 2007

Notice
No responsibility is assumed by the publisher for any injury and/or damage to
persons or property as a matter of products liability, negligence or otherwise,
or from any use or operation of any methods, products, instructions or
ideas contained in the material herein. Because of rapid advances in the
medical sciences, in particular, independent verification of diagnoses and
drug dosages should be made

British Library Cataloguing in Publication Data
A catalogue record for this book is available from the British Library

Library of Congress Cataloging-in-Publication Data
A catalog record for this book is available from the Library of Congress

ISBN-13: 978-0-7506-6798-2
ISBN-10: 0-7506-6798-2

For information on all Butterworth-Heinemann publications
visit our web site at books.elsevier.com

Typeset by Integra Software Services Pvt. Ltd, Pondicherry, India
www.integra-india.com

Printed and bound in the United Kingdom
Transferred to Digital Print 2011

Contents

Contents

Introduction

Many funds have decided to concentrate on their role as investment managers and have elected to outsource as much of the additional work structure, particularly operational work. Also the "newer" funds like hedge funds are structured in such a way that the support roles like custody and administration tend to be handled by specialist organisations, prime brokers and fund administrators.

These roles are important as in reducing almost completely the need for the "fund manager", in this sense the sponsor/owner, to be involved in anything but investment decision-making; and the setting up of new hedge funds is made staggeringly easy. This may go some way in explaining the significant growth in these funds in recent years (hedge funds are not a new phenomena).

However, fund administration has evolved from a relatively humble beginning where the primary role was that of calculating the value of the assets in the fund so that a price for the investors wanting to buy or sell shares or units in the fund could be established. Today a fund administrator may have roles related to everything from setting up the fund to risk management and compliance roles. The administrator is very much monitoring the fund to ensure that the actions of the investment manager are in line with the objectives of the fund, the regulatory environment applicable to the fund, the tax situation affecting the fund and the client service role between the fund and its investors.

As a result some of the functions previously carried out by specialist firms have been absorbed into the fund administration role, particularly within the larger fund administrators. Transfer agency/fund registrar services for instance are provided as part of fund administration services by some companies. However specialists can and do survive, providing bespoke services to their clients.

In some ways the fund administration business has evolved in a similar way to custody services. Consolidation, expanding range of services, competition, increased costs and investment have all impacted on the business.

This expansion of funds and the role of the fund administrator is not without its problems. Some financial centres like Dublin have witnessed huge growth within a short time frame. This can obviously lead to strains on the infrastructure and the community not only in small offshore locations but also in larger locals like Dublin and Luxembourg. Shortage of experienced personnel is an inevitable consequence of the development of fund administration services in a developing financial centre. This is made more critical by the need for skill sets in more and more diverse products and strategies, particularly in the hedge fund arena. Another factor is that the large organisations can move their entire operations function dealing with the administration of funds and other operations-based functions to these localities putting even greater pressure on the recruitment environment.

We can add increased workflow to the list of evolution of the fund administrator's role. Many of the funds that appoint external administrators have been small funds like private funds, hedge funds, etc and many of them were closed funds. These funds by nature had, relative to retail mutual funds, far fewer requirements in terms of reporting, etc. As a result many would calculate the NAV of the fund perhaps monthly, some even less frequently. Today many of the hedge funds are seeking to be included in funds of hedge funds and these in turn are attractive vehicles for other funds to invest in. As a result the NAV needs to be calculated daily if the wide appeal is to be maintained. Given the types of products these funds might be investing in, the relatively straightforward NAV calculation by the administrator becomes, when needed on a daily basis, somewhat of a nightmare.

If we also consider the greater sophistication in the use of products and strategies and therefore the need for product and market knowledge then the whole administration process, not just valuations, becomes a much more demanding function.

Reporting to investors and the manager, fund set-up, monitoring compliance and managing risk have all become more and more high profile issues and the fund administrator has had to respond by developing and providing the kind of support and services that the managers require.

We should not assume that all of this change is hedge fund-driven or that it applies only to hedge funds. Hedge funds have indeed grown significantly so that today we have some 8000 hedge funds worldwide and an awesome amount under management in those funds, some sources putting the figure in 2005 at $1500 billion.

Europe alone has some 1500 hedge funds, most of them in London, with funds under management of some $300 billion, an increase of 18 per cent over the previous year.

We can get the picture of the overall size of the investment fund industry by noting that the Investment Managers Association state that "between them IMA's members manage over £2 trillion of assets".

The changes in regulation of mutual funds and other collective investment schemes through the various EU Directives on derivatives use and operational risk have also required the fund administrators to evaluate their potential role and opportunities.

One thing is for sure, the changes will continue; and so, as long as wealth continues to be created, will the growth in the number of funds. Each one will need an administrator!

Europe alone has some 1500 hedge funds, most of them in London, with funds under management of some $300 billion, an increase of 18 per cent over the previous year.

We can get the picture of the overall size of the investment fund industry by noting that the Investment Managers Association state that 'its over then IMA's members, manage over £2 trillion of assets'.

The changes in regulation of mutual funds and other collective investment schemes through the various EU Directives on derivatives use and operational risk have also required the fund administrators to evaluate their potential role and opportunities.

One thing is for sure, the changes will continue, and so, as long as wealth continues to be created, will the growth in the number of funds. Each one will need an administrator.

1

Understanding the investment environment

Investment, like the administrator's role, has undergone much change. The pressure on funds to perform against an increasingly large competitive market for investors' cash has had several effects.

First, the investment time horizons have shortened so that the turnover in the asset classes within the portfolio has increased. Secondly, fund managers are looking for greater returns and are facing more risk in the process of doing so. The administrator is having an increasingly hard time trying to calculate NAVs and at the same time monitor the fund's activities for compliance with the trust deeds, mandates and marketing regulation.

Fundamentally the investment environment follows a route from research through execution of trades, onto settlement and safekeeping of the assets and administration. From there various reports and data on positions, exposure, performance of the investments, etc. feeds into research and so the cycle starts again (see Figure 1.1).

The flow as shown in Figure 1.1 is generic for all funds and obviously the precise actions, decisions, functions, tasks and controls will vary from one type of fund to another. Let us look at some of these fund structures.

Investment funds

Investment funds go under a variety of names. These names reflect the type of investment objectives and the investor that the fund is aimed at. These fund titles can be:

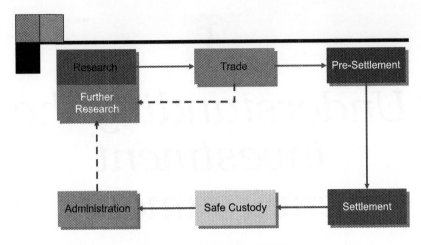

Figure 1.1 Investment Cycle

- Institutional funds
- Retail funds
- Pension funds
- Life funds
- Hedge funds
- Private Equity funds
- Venture Capital funds.

Each of these funds is designed to achieve particular outcomes and the investment manager is required to deliver the performance the investor expects. The term 'institutional fund' refers to funds set up by companies for either employees' benefits, i.e. pensions, or for sale in the retail market to investors. These are either managed by the company concerned or alternatively the management is outsourced to a fund management company.

By way of contrast hedge funds may be private funds set up and managed by individuals for themselves or for sale to qualifying investors. Currently in most jurisdictions hedge funds cannot be sold to the "ordinary" investor. Qualifying investors for hedge funds are "market professionals", i.e. they either have a comprehensive knowledge of the markets and the risk associated with investing in different types of funds, or alternatively they have the ability to demonstrate they have such wealth that they could withstand, should it happen, the loss of their entire investment. It must be noted that not all hedge funds carry high risk nor do they routinely lose the investors' capital. The types of strategies and products they are permitted to use do however mean that unlike say a mutual saving fund which must be highly diversified and use relatively risk-free strategies, they can take significant exposures which if the market moves against them could result in the loss of all the capital of the fund.

Investment funds themselves, for instance pension funds, can invest some of their capital into hedge funds but the amount, if any, is governed by regulation and the mandate of the fund.

Structure of funds

Investment funds are generally structured as either "open-ended" or "closed". These terms refer to the shares or units in the fund that investors can hold. Shares are issued by investment companies and units by funds set up as trusts, hence the term "unit trusts".

Types of funds are looked at in more detail in later chapters but a summary of the types of structures is important here if we are to understand the investment environment.

A closed fund has a finite number of shares or units in existence whereas an open-ended fund creates or cancels shares/units as investors look to purchase or sell their holding. The size in terms of the number of investors and the holding they have of an open-ended fund can therefore increase or decrease depending on the attractiveness of the fund to investors.

Unit trusts

Unit trusts were created in the United States as long ago as 1931. These unit trusts were "closed" trusts and once the initial investment decisions had been made they were rarely altered. This passive investment process had the advantage of certainty for the investor – they knew for what the fund was invested in and that it did not change – but the disadvantage was its inability to adapt to market conditions and opportunities.

Unit trusts became popular investment vehicles for the public in the UK but the characteristic of the unit trust had changed considerably by then. As collective investment schemes the unit trusts were also mostly open-ended so that the number of units in existence increased or decreased depending on the investors' demands to buy new units or redeem their existing units. The unit trusts were also actively managed and whilst many of them were securities-based, some unit trusts were issued that invested in other products like warrants, property and money markets.

Unit trusts were also created that had different classes of units, accumulation and distribution which related to the income that was generated from the assets. Accumulation units re-invested the income whilst the distribution units paid the income to the investor periodically, often annually.

By being created under trust law rather than company law, the assets of the fund are held on behalf of the investors by a trustee.

Trustee

The trustee monitors the activities of the investment or fund manager to make certain that the investments are in line with the trust deed. The trustee owns the assets of the fund, not the fund manager and if there are more buyers than sellers of the units in the fund it is the trustee who will, on request by the fund manager, create more units, or the reverse if there are more sellers than buyers.

Trust deed

The trust deed sets out the terms under which the trust is established and specifies the investment objectives, products and markets permitted, constraints on investments and the amount of risk the fund manager can establish in the portfolio.

Fund manager

The fund manager is the firm and/or person making the investment decisions. Many large unit trusts are managed by investment companies. Employees working for the company as fund managers deal with particular funds and make decisions based on:

1. The trust deed
2. The fund management company's view of markets and products
3. The asset allocation profile of the fund
4. Selecting individual assets to be held in the portfolio
5. Adjusting the assets to reflect market conditions and change.

The fund management company will be responsible for marketing and sales of units in the trusts for which it acts as investment/fund manager for and makes its money by charging fees to investors. These fees are based on an initial fee paid when the units are first purchased and management fees related to the function of the manager in making investment decisions and running the fund.

Some funds are what is called "multi-manager" funds and this can involve more than one management firm being responsible for managing parts of the portfolio. For example manager A may manage equities and manager B fixed income investments within the fund. Equally there could be two managers from different firms managing the equity part of the portfolio on a percentage basis, i.e. fund manager A manages 60 per cent and manager B 40 per cent.

Custodian

The trustee may appoint a custodian to hold the assets of the fund in safekeeping and to deal with the settlement of transactions undertaken by the manager.

Investment company

Many investment companies have broadly the same structures as unit trusts. There are closed and open-ended investment companies, have managers who take the investment decisions for the funds, issue and redeem shares with investors, can be single or multi-manager companies, have different classes of shares and will have a depositary and a custodian.

As these funds are set up as companies under company law there is no trust to manage. The assets of the fund are owned by the investment company and the investors own shares in the company that give them various rights to participation similar to shareholders in any company.

Responsibility for the performance of the company lie with the Board of Directors with a designated title for one of them in UK investment companies of Associate Corporate Director (ACD). The ACD is essentially the same as the fund or investment. The monitoring of the way in which the ACD operates the fund is carried out by the Depository who broadly speaking does the same role as the trustee in a unit trust.

Investment companies go by various names depending on the country in which they are established. For example we have Open-Ended Investment Companies (OEICs) and Investment Companies with Variable Capital (ICVCs), Mutual Funds, SICAVs, etc.

Authorised and unauthorised funds

Funds are either authorised or not by the local regulator for sale to retail investors.

As noted earlier, unit trusts and investment funds are *collective investment schemes* whereby investors' money is pooled and managed as one amount by the investment/fund manager with each investor having a share in the assets in the portfolio.

Authorised funds must comply not only with the trust deed if there is one but also with the terms given in the prospectus or other authorising document such as the Scheme Particulars that must be available to the investor before they purchase shares or units, but also with the Regulations applicable to firms conducting investment business.

Funds that are authorised by the regulator can be sold to the general public; those that are not authorised can be sold only to certain types of investor, usually the ones that can prove either market knowledge and expertise or certain levels of wealth or both.

Onshore and offshore funds

Funds are established in either onshore or offshore jurisdictions. The main reason for this is the tax and regulatory environment and the target investor base.

Offshore funds are neither "tax free" nor "unregulated". However the rate of tax applied to the funds' activities may be more attractive in an offshore locality and likewise there may be a less onerous regulatory environment applying to the activities of the fund. For some investors this may be important as they want both tax efficiency in their investments and accept possibly less protection from the regulator. Offshore funds are therefore often "unauthorised" for sale to the general public and can only be sold to what is often referred to as "qualifying investors".

"Offshore" today can actually refer to onshore localities such as Dublin and Luxembourg where special "offshore" areas have been created. Other offshore locations where funds are registered include:

* Jersey
* Guernsey
* Isle of Man
* Bermuda
* Cayman
* Bahamas
* British Virgin Isles

Other locations are beginning to develop the offshore facility for funds such as Mauritius.

Portfolio investment

Funds are established with investment objectives in mind.

This is reflected in the title of funds, for example UK Small Caps would indicate that the fund invests in small capitalised UK-based companies. A Global Income Fund would suggest that the fund invests in assets that will generate income, dividends, interest, etc. Some funds are mixed so that they are designed to deliver both capital growth and income.

The manager therefore has the guideline for what the fund is investing in, however there are further guidelines and objectives.

The fund will have a target for the return it will deliver to the investor. Often this is in simplistic terms a percentage return; for instance a fund may have a target of growth or income return of 10 per cent per annum. This is sometimes set against a benchmark so, for instance, the fund might be expected to return X per cent more than an index such as the FTSE 100 or the S & P 500.

Fund managers may also operate within a benchmark allocation of what is called 'asset classes and targets' (see Figure 1.2).

In Figure 1.2 the portfolio has what is called a 'strategic asset allocation' split across equities, bonds and cash. If the fund has received a subscription of say £100,000 the manager will invest this £60,000 in acceptable equities, £30,000 in acceptable bonds and £10,000 in acceptable cash instruments. The selection of the actual instruments and securities is down to the manager and the target is to at least equal the indices shown.

In some funds the manager may have the ability to take opportunities in the markets through what is known as tactical asset allocation. Here the manager may be able to deviate away from the strategic asset allocation by up to say 10 per cent. In this case the manager could structure the portfolio as 70 per cent equities, 20 per cent bonds and 10 per cent cash; however the target benchmark returns are still the same. If by deviating away from the strategic asset allocation the manager underperforms, i.e. generates less return than the indices, questions will obviously be asked by both investors and the chief investment officer!

Performance measurement is looked at in more detail in Chapter 8.

Asset Class	Strategic Asset Allocation	Benchmark
Equities	60%	FT All Share
Bonds	30%	FT Gilt Index
Cash	10%	Merrill Lynch Index

Figure 1.2 Performance

Markets and investments

Fund managers must have somewhere to invest the money contributed to the fund by the investors.

In most cases the money is invested through the capital markets in either the purchase of equity (shares) in companies listed on stock exchanges or new issues (public offerings) of shares on stock exchanges, debt instruments like fixed income bonds, floating rate notes, etc. issued by governments, companies and other government agencies or local authorities like local or county councils, etc. and in cash or what is called "near cash" instruments like treasury bills.

The precise instruments that are used depend on the types of fund and what it is permitted to use.

For example any fund allowed to invest in government bonds could invest in the bonds issued by the governments of the G7 countries like the US, UK, France, Germany, Japan, etc. However retail funds may be restricted and not permitted to take the risk of investing in the bonds of emerging markets where although the income return is higher there is a greater risk of the fund losing its money if the issuer defaults on a payment or redemption of the bond.

Likewise a hedge fund which can assume far greater risk than an authorised unit trust can "gear" or "leverage" the portfolio's exposure by using products like derivatives where they can acquire a much greater exposure for the money invested than a unit trust can by investing the same amount in shares.

Example

Hedge Fund has £50,000 to invest in BP shares which are currently trading at £5. The manager wants to gear the exposure so instead of buying 10,000 shares he or she looks at the BP options listed on the exchange and sees that the price of the BP July 550 call options is 50p. Each option contract is based on 1000 shares with a delivery price if the option is exercised at 550p. The cost of 1 contract is therefore £500 (1000 x 50p). The hedge fund manager buys 100 contracts for a total of £50,000. However the exposure to the shares is actually 100 x 1000 = 100,000 shares.

The mutual fund manager cannot gear the fund so he or she buys 10,000 shares.

Let us say that BP's share price jumps to £6 and the options move up to £1.

The mutual fund manager has a healthy £10,000 profit.

The hedge fund manager can sell the options at £1 and has gained 50p per option contract or 100,000 shares x 50p = £50,000 profit for exactly the same outlay as the mutual fund manager and has no costs associated with buying shares like stamp duty!!

Of course there is a good reason why the mutual fund investor is protected against gearing the exposure.

Suppose BP fell to £4. By expiry the options are worthless as no one will pay £5.50 for shares that are only worth £4. The hedge fund has lost £50,000.

The mutual fund has lost £10,000 but owns the shares and can wait until they rise in price. The mutual fund as owners of shares will also receive any dividend BP may pay whilst the hedge fund has no dividend income as it owns options not shares.

It is important to understand the restrictions and guidelines that the fund manager must follow because there are so many possibilities in the markets that a fund manager could use.

It is also important to remember that restrictions can apply to how much exposure the fund can have to a type of product, issuer, specific security, etc., so whilst a manager may be able to buy shares in a company the fund may be restricted to holding no more than say 15 per cent of the funds total value in any one share.

The following are some examples of restrictions.

UCITS III – The Product Directive

The Product Directive expands the range and type of financial instruments permitted under the 1985 Directive to include the following:

- Transferable Securities and Money market instruments.
- Bank Deposits.
- Units of other investment funds.
- Financial derivative instruments.
- Index tracking funds.

In addition, the definition of "transferable securities" has been amended and is defined as:

- shares in companies and other securities equivalent to shares in companies;

- bonds and other forms of securitised debt; and
- any other negotiable securities which carry the right to acquire any such transferable securities by subscription or exchange.

This definition does not include techniques and instruments used for efficient portfolio management.

Aggregate limits

The Directive applies individual investment restriction limits to each financial instrument. These individual investment restriction limits are subject to overall combined limits of 20 per cent and 35 per cent of the NAV of a UCITS Fund.

A UCITS Fund is permitted to invest an overall combined limit of 35 per cent of its assets in the following investments:

- transferable securities and money market instruments;
- deposits; and/or
- derivative instruments issued by or made with the same body.

A maximum limit of 20 per cent of the NAV of a UCITS Fund applies to the following investments:

- transferable securities and money market instruments;
- deposits; and/or
- exposures arising from OTC derivative transactions issued by or made with the same body.

In summary the 20 per cent limit applies to combined investments including OTC derivatives whilst the 35 per cent limit is an overall limit that refers to derivatives traded on a regulated market as well as OTC derivatives. Group companies are regarded as single issuers for the purposes of calculating individual and aggregate restriction limits.

Transferable Securities and Money Market Instruments

Money market instruments are described in the Product Directive as instruments normally dealt in on the money market that are liquid and have a value that can be accurately determined at any time.

A UCITS may invest a maximum of 5 per cent of its assets in transferable securities and money market instruments issued by a single issuer. Member States may increase this limit to 10 per cent but the total value of positions in excess of 5 per cent must not exceed 40 per cent of NAV; member states may permit a UCITS to invest a maximum of 35 per cent of its assets in transferable securities and money market instruments issued or guaranteed by an EU Member State or its local authorities, by a non-Member State or by public international bodies to which one or more Member States belong; subject to certain conditions a UCITS may invest up to 100 per cent of its net assets in different transferable securities and money market instruments issued or guaranteed by any Member State its local authorities non Member State or public international body of which one or more Member States are members.

Where money market instruments are not traded on a regulated market, investment is only permitted if the issuer is regulated and provided that the money market instruments are:

- issued or guaranteed by a central, regional or local authority or central bank of a Member State;
- issued by an undertaking any securities of which are dealt in on a regulated market;
- issued or guaranteed by an establishment subject to prudential supervision in accordance with criteria defined by the European Union;
- issued by other bodies belonging to the categories approved by the UCITS' competent authority.

Bank Deposits

Deposits with credit institutions are permitted provided the credit institution has its registered office in a EU Member State or, if located in a non-Member State, it is subject to equivalent prudential rules of a EU Member State. The deposits must be repayable on demand or have the right to be withdrawn and may have a maturity of up to 12 months. Not more than 20 per cent of the UCITS' investments in deposits may be placed with the same credit institution (including the UCITS' custodian).

Financial Derivatives Instruments

Under the 1985 Directive UCITS were permitted to invest in derivatives for the purposes of efficient portfolio management only.

The Directive still permits UCITS to invest in derivatives for efficient portfolio management. However, the Product Directive extends the nature of the investments to include financial derivative instruments including equivalent cash settled instruments dealt in on a regulated market and/or over the counter derivatives ("OTC derivatives").

The conditions and limits set out in the Product Directive for derivatives must apply even where derivatives are used for efficient portfolio management or are embedded in transferable securities or money market instruments.

The conditions set out in the Product Directive in relation to the calculation of the exposure of derivative instruments include the following:

- the global exposure relating to the derivative instruments must not exceed the total NAV of the UCITS Fund;
- the exposure must be calculated taking into account the current value of the underlying assets, the counterparty risk, future market movements and the time available to liquidate the positions; and
- in the case of OTC derivatives, the exposure to a single counterparty must not exceed 10 per cent of NAV if the counterparty is a EU credit institution or equivalent, or 5 per cent of NAV in other cases.

For OTC derivative transactions, the counterparties must be subject to prudential supervision, the OTC derivatives must be subject to reliable and verifiable valuation on a daily basis and must be capable of being closed out at any time. The permitted underlying investments of OTC derivatives include financial indices, interest rates, foreign exchange rates or currencies in which the UCITS Fund may invest according to its constitutional documents. The selection of financial indices as underlying investments for OTC derivatives is a management technique. However, competent authorities may require the assets underlying the financial indices to be assets that a UCITS Fund may directly invest in pursuant to the Product Directive.

Special risk management reporting to the competent authority is required in relation to investment in derivatives. A UCITS must demonstrate that it has appropriate risk management controls and valuation procedures in place. The risk management processes to be applied are not, however, laid down in the directive and will, therefore, be determined by Member States on an individual basis. It should be noted that where financial derivatives do not form the main part of a fund's investments but are, rather, employed for the purposes of efficient portfolio management, these risk management procedures will still apply and will override any previous rules for derivatives used for efficient portfolio management. It should also be noted that short sales continue to be prohibited as investments for UCITS Funds.

Funds of Funds

Under the Product Directive, a fund of funds can now qualify for UCITS status subject to the following conditions:

- a fund of funds, established as a UCITS, is permitted to invest up to 10 per cent of its NAV in a single UCITS or equivalent, provided the equivalent structure is subject to risk diversification, leverage and regulatory controls similar to that of a UCITS. Member States are permitted under the Product Directive to increase this 10 per cent limit to 20 per cent;
- total investment in funds other than UCITS must not exceed 30 per cent of the NAV of the fund;
- a UCITS may not acquire more than 25 per cent of the units of any single UCITS; and
- a UCITS fund of funds may not invest in an underlying fund if that underlying fund is permitted to invest more than 10 per cent of its NAV in other funds of funds.

Index Tracking Funds

In the case of funds, the aim of which is to replicate an index, an investment limit of 20 per cent of the NAV of the UCITS Fund applies where the investment consists of shares and/or debt securities issued by the same body. This limit may be increased by Member States to 35 per cent where it is justified by exceptional market conditions. The index must be sufficiently diversified, represent an adequate benchmark and be published in an appropriate manner. It is the responsibility of each Member State to assess the suitability of a particular index as the basis for a UCITS.

Use of Subsidiaries

The Product Directive provides that a UCITS may have a subsidiary for the purposes of management, advice or marketing, with regard to the repurchase of units, in the country where the subsidiary is located. Although there is some uncertainty as to whether certain existing subsidiary structures will be permitted in the future, it seems clear that the Product Directive removes the opportunity which was previously available for a UCITS to establish a subsidiary company in a non-EU jurisdiction for the purposes of efficient portfolio management, including access to tax treaties.

Source: Ernst & Young; UCITS III A Practical Guide.

Investment drivers

Investors come from all backgrounds and financial standing.

Their savings and investments are usually made with some objective in mind, a pension for example. Some just have spare cash and want to potentially earn more than just leaving it on deposit at a bank.

Investment levels do fluctuate. When cash is tight because of high interest rates, personal debt or maybe job insecurity there will obviously be less inflow of cash into investment funds. But not everyone is affected in the same way so whilst some may be short of money, others have money to invest.

So whilst inflow may fluctuate there is a general increase in investment spread across a greater number of possible investment choices.

The general drivers behind the investment environment we have to day are

- Increasing wealth as economies around the world grow
- Sophistication of investors who seek better rewards
- A shortening of the investment timescale
- A greater understanding of and preparedness to take risk in investment for higher returns
- Global access to markets, products and opportunities
- Growth in hedge funds
- Growth in alternative investments (not just using equities and bonds but more innovative and diverse products).

Changes to the regulations affecting investment is also having a major impact on how investment products are being designed and investment decisions are being made. The greater opportunity for investment managers to take some degree of risk in search of higher return as implied in the UCITS III Directive is leading to potentially greater use of over-the-counter derivatives in portfolios. Commodities are also being incorporated into mainstream portfolios as a "new" asset class.

Changes to tax laws can also have an impact on the type of investment and structure of fund. For example in the EU a new requirement regarding the taxation of interest income came into place in 2005 called the 'European Savings Tax Directive'. It affected offshore financial centres where an EU resident had their investments.

The following is an example of the requirements for establishing a collective investment fund in Jersey. Readers should note that other jurisdictions will have different requirements and that in all jurisdictions, including Jersey, the requirements are subject to change.

A guide to establishing a collective investment fund operation in Jersey

The Requirements of Legislation

The two principal laws

The establishment and operation of collective investment funds in Jersey is governed principally by two pieces of legislation, namely, the Control of Borrowing (Jersey) Law, 1947 as amended, (the "Borrowing Law") and the Collective Investment Funds (Jersey) Law, 1988 as amended, (the "CIF Law"). Although the scopes of the two statutes overlap, in practice a collective investment fund with a limited number of investors will probably be governed by the Borrowing Law alone; whereas if the units of the fund are offered on a more public basis, that fund will be regulated under the CIF Law. Together the two statutes provide the framework for appropriate investor protection whilst retaining the flexibility to adapt quickly to changing market conditions.

Responsibility for the administration of these Laws rests with the Jersey Financial Services Commission (the "Commission").

The Borrowing Law

The Borrowing Law provides for the supervision in the Island of the raising of money, the issue of securities and the circulation of offers for the subscription, sale or exchange of securities. Subordinate legislation made pursuant to the Borrowing Law, namely, the Control of Borrowing (Jersey) Order, 1958 as amended, gives the Commission control, inter alia, over the raising of investment capital. The issue of shares or units in a collective investment fund and the circulation of prospectuses and sales literature requires the consent of the Commission. The majority of collective investment fund offers will therefore fall to be supervised under the Borrowing Law.

Where the collective investment fund is also subject to the CIF Law, the issue of a consent under the Borrowing Law should just be a formality.

When considering an application for consent, the Borrowing Law requires the Commission to have regard to the need to protect the integrity of the Island in commercial and financial matters and the best economic interests of the Island.

The CIF Law

1. Testing for Applicability

To determine whether or not a proposal falls within the CIF Law, three questions need to be asked:

1.1. Is it a "Collective Investment Fund"?

Article 3 of the CIF Law defines a collective investment fund.

Briefly, it is any scheme or arrangement for the investment of money which:

a) has as its object, or one of its objects, the collective investment of capital acquired by means of an "offer to the public" (see below) of units for subscription, sale or exchange; and
b) operates on the principle of risk spreading, or issues units continuously, or the units are redeemable continuously at the request of the holder and out of the assets of the fund.

"Offers to the Public"

Under paragraph 3 of Article 3, there are six criteria all of which must be satisfied for an offer of units to be considered to be not an offer to the public:

- the offer must be addressed to an identifiable category of persons; and
- the offer must be directly communicated to those persons by the offerer or his appointed agent; and
- they must have sufficient information to be able to evaluate the offer; and there must not be more than 50 such offers; and
- the units must not be listed on any stock exchange within one year of the offer being made.

1.2. Who are the functionaries?

Article 4, together with the Schedule to the CIF Law, determines who is to be treated as a functionary of a fund.

The Schedule to the CIF Law lists some 17 functions. They include functions such as Manager, Administrator, Registrar, Investment Manager, Investment Adviser, Distributor, Subscription Agent, Redemption Agent, Trustee, Custodian, Depository.

1.3. When is a permit required?

In summary, Article 5 requires that if a person wishes to carry on or hold himself out as carrying on, one of the defined functions in Article 4, in or from within Jersey, then he can only do so once the Commission has granted him a permit to do so. If the person concerned is a Jersey company, or Jersey limited partnership then a permit will be required regardless of where the function is carried on.

Under subordinate legislation, exemptions from the requirements of Article 5 apply to certain persons carrying on insurance business. If the answer to all three questions is yes then permits will be required.

N.B. – This guide is concerned only with collective investment funds established in Jersey. However, it should be noted that for a fund to fall within Article 3 it need not necessarily be domiciled in Jersey. Thus, it is possible to be a functionary to a non-Jersey fund and still require a permit under the CIF Law.

2. Two Classes of Funds

The CIF Law provides that different fund classes may be established, and that subordinate legislation may be introduced for any such class. At present only one class has been introduced, the Recognized Funds class. All other funds under the CIF Law are therefore unclassified funds.

2.1. Recognized Funds

A "Recognized Fund" is one which complies with all the relevant requirements of the subordinate legislation under the CIF Law applicable to this class of fund (the "Recognized Fund legislation"), and has therefore been granted a Recognized Fund certificate.

The Recognized Fund legislation, which is modelled on the corresponding UK legislation, was introduced in order to demonstrate that the regulation of Recognized Funds in Jersey ensures investor protection that is at least equivalent to that afforded investors in the UK under the Financial Services and Markets Act 2000 (the 'FSMA'). As a result, the UK authorities have declared that Jersey is a 'Designated Territory' and any fund which has been granted a Recognized Fund certificate may seek authorisation under Section 270 of the FSMA to market directly to the general public in the UK. Only three other territories have been granted this status.

Under the Recognized Fund legislation, a fund may only take the form of a unit trust or an open-ended investment company.

The legislation prescribes the requirements applicable to most aspects of the fund's structure and operation, and the contents of the prospectus.

In addition, there are requirements applicable to certain of the functionaries (particularly the manager and the custodian or trustee). All of these must be complied with for the relevant Recognized Fund permit to be granted.

2.2. Unclassified Funds

Although the requirements applicable to an unclassified fund are broadly the same as for recognized funds, they are not prescribed in statute other than in relation to the prospectuses of open-ended unclassified funds. An unclassified fund established in Jersey may be open-ended or close-ended and may have a corporate structure or be a unit trust or a limited partnership.

It is the Commission's policy that each unclassified fund is regulated to an extent and in a manner considered to be appropriate to the nature of the particular fund. This involves negotiations with the promoter and/or his professional adviser, following scrutiny of all the documentation and other information associated with the unclassified fund.

This policy has been maintained and developed over the years in order to facilitate innovation by the industry in Jersey and enable the Commission to be responsive to it whilst still protecting both the investors and the Island's excellent reputation as an international finance centre. Regardless of what type of permit is applied for, when considering an application for a permit, the Commission is required by the CIF Law to have regard to the protection of the public and to the best economic interests of the Island and to this end must consider the function to be performed by the applicant, the reputation of the applicant and the collective investment fund to which his function relates. Also the Commission must take into account any other functionaries of the collective investment fund to which the application relates.

Application Procedures *Top*

Introduction

The distinction between those funds which fall to be supervised under the CIF Law and those under the Borrowing Law is often not that significant for the purpose of making an application. What is more relevant to the Commission is the sophistication of the proposed investors. The more a fund is targeted towards investors who are institutions or individuals experienced in investment matters, the more flexible the Commission can be in its regulatory requirements, relying instead on adequate disclosure. There are, however, certain procedural requirements that may have to be complied with under the CIF Law which may not necessarily be there under the Borrowing Law.

The review activity for all applications under both the CIF Law and the Borrowing Law involves three distinct stages. In addition, before approaching the first of these, promoters or their representatives often find it helpful to discuss their intentions on an informal basis with the Authorisation area of the Commission.

1. Initial review stage

At this stage, Authorisation needs to have a submission, in writing, giving:

1.1. The identity of the promoters (promoting companies and any group of which they are a part) together with their most recent report and accounts and any further background information which will enable Authorisation to establish their stature, reputation and track record;

Appendix A contains a copy of the policy statement applied by Authorisation when evaluating the stature of a promoter of a collective investment fund.

1.2. Similar information will be required regarding other functionaries to the fund, where the function performed is considered to be material unless that information is readily available to Authorisation (for example, if the functionary holds a permit under the CIF Law in respect of a similar function performed for another fund).

1.3. Also required will be general information regarding the fund, its proposed investments, its structure (equivalent in its nature and extent to information normally contained in the main parts of the prospectus), the nature of the investors and the minimum investment.

Applicants are normally required to complete a formal checklist itemising each of these matters.

The initial review stage will conclude with Authorisation writing a letter to the applicants indicating whether or not the application can be proceeded with subject to the Commission being satisfied with the structure and documents of the proposal in due course.

2. Document review stage

This stage involves the detailed examination of the structure and draft documents for the fund which should be submitted with the completed application forms (including the prescribed fees) for the required permits.

2.1 Recognized Funds

For the review of a Recognized Fund, Authorisation will require a copy of a draft of each of the following documents:

- the prospectus;
- the trust instrument, or the memorandum and articles of association (as applicable);
- the fund rules, if any;
- all material contracts (typically those listed in the prospectus);
- any resolutions of the board of directors on matters such as investment limits, borrowing powers, valuation regulation, etc.

There must also be submitted a certificate signed by an advocate or solicitor of the Royal Court to the effect that the memorandum, articles of association, management agreement and custodian agreement, or the trust instrument (as applicable), comply with such of the requirements of the Collective Investment Funds (Recognized Funds) (Rules) (Jersey) Order, 2003 as relate to their contents.

Because the content of the prospectus and the manner in which the fund may operate are prescribed by the recognized fund legislation, there is very little room for discretion by the Commission on the structure and operation of such funds.

2.2 Unclassified funds

When making an application for an unclassified fund permit, the completed application form(s) (including the prescribed fees), should normally be accompanied by a draft copy of each of the same documents as those described for a recognized fund permit (see above).

However, instead of a certificate from an advocate, the documents should be accompanied by a "document review checklist". This lists all the regulatory matters which the Commission will consider (as applicable), during the review. A more detailed description of each item on the checklist, and other matters relevant to open-ended unclassified funds is contained in the relevant guide, a copy of which is available from Authorisation on request). For each item on the checklist, the applicant is expected to identify the location in the constitutive documents where the requirement is addressed and, if the documents are partly or wholly non-compliant, to give reasons why this is.

It is important to note that the Commission does take a flexible stance with regard to unclassified funds. The requirements addressed by the checklist are those considered appropriate to open-ended funds offered to the most inexperienced investor. The more the Commission is satisfied that the fund will only be available to experienced investors, the more relaxed will be the approach taken with regard to a number of the regulatory requirements in the checklist, relying instead on adequate disclosure of the risks etc. in the prospectus.

2.3 Borrowing Law funds

In the case of applications that fall only under the Borrowing Law, the Commission will take a more relaxed view with regard to investor protection matters concentrating more on adequate disclosure of risks in the prospectus and that what is to be done is consistent with protecting the Island's reputation.

The review of this category of fund will normally involve only examination of the draft prospectus. No other documents should therefore be submitted unless they are expressly requested.

3. Formal licensing stage

In the case of permits under the CIF Law (recognized or unclassified), Authorisation would wish to be provided with certified copies of all the material contracts, the memorandum and articles/trust instrument including fund rules and board resolutions and a copy of the prospectus in final form.

In the case of consents under the Borrowing Law, a copy of the prospectus in final form will be required. No other documents will normally be needed. The formal licensing stage will conclude either with the issue of permits, under the CIF Law and/or consent under the Borrowing Law. It is usual that the permits (or if there are none, the consent under the Borrowing Law) will be subject to one or more conditions.

Timescales

The time taken to carry out each of the stages of the review process is dependent upon a number of variables and therefore it is impossible to indicate such times with complete accuracy.

The Commission recommends that two weeks be allowed for Authorisation to respond to an application at the initial review stage, providing the area receives all the information necessary to come to a view, particularly with regard to any promoters new to the Island.

At the document review stage, four weeks should be allowed from the time Authorisation receives the completed application forms and the draft documents to the issue of any comments there may be as a result of the detailed review.

The time taken by Authorisation for both these stages will often be well within those indicated above, particularly for funds subject only to the Borrowing Law. In cases of genuine urgency, much shorter timescales are possible and the team will always do its best to meet any reasonable targets of which it has been given notice.

For all types of funds, the formal licensing stage rarely takes more than two or three days.

Note: The full guide is available at the JFSC website: www.jerseyfsc.org

Source: Jersey Financial Service Commission.

Another example of the impact regulation can have is the Registration of UCITS.

The following is an illustration of the borrowing and investment restrictions that can apply to funds.

The illustration is taken from a supplement to the 2006 Guide to Fund Management which can be found on the website of The International Financial Law Review, **www.iflr.com**. The article is referring to lending to Irish-domiciled funds and the investment and borrowing restrictions talked about here may differ in other jurisdictions and for other types of funds.

Types of funds and borrowing and investment restrictions

The applicable borrowing restrictions depend on whether or not the fund is a Undertaking for Collective Investments in Transferable Secuirties (UCITS) and, if it is not a UCITS, the type of non-UCITS investor targeted. Of the 960 (about) Irish-domiciled, regulated investment funds, about 320 are UCITS. The non-UCITS funds are split as follows: 203 are authorized as retail funds, 136 are authorized as professional investor funds and 200 are authorized as qualifying investor funds.

Generally, the more unsophisticated the target investor, the more restrictive will be the borrowing capacity and the more extensive will be the investment restrictions.

UCITS

UCITS are diversified open-ended investment funds whose object must be to invest capital raised from the public in transferable securities. These include shares, other securities equivalent to shares, bonds, securitized debt, money market instruments, units or shares in other collective investment schemes and liquid financial assets (deposits with maturities of 12 months or less, standardized derivatives, and certain OTC derivatives). UCITS are open-ended vehicles insofar as investors must generally be entitled to redeem their shares or units on request at least once every two weeks. UCITS are investment vehicles established under the EU UCITS directives that were implemented into law in Ireland by the European Communities (UCITS) Regulations 1989 and 2003. Once a UCITS is authorized in one member state, subject to certain notification requirements, it cannot be prohibited from selling or promoting the sale of its shares or units to the public in any other member state. In addition, there are limited restrictions on the type of investor to whom interests in the fund can be sold.

The borrowing powers of UCITS funds are restricted. The borrowings of a UCITS cannot exceed 10 per cent of its net asset value and it must be on a temporary basis. It may borrow up to 10 per cent of its net asset value to acquire property required for the purpose of its business but where it does so the total borrowings of the UCITS may not exceed 15 per cent of its net asset value. This borrowing power has rarely been used; because the borrowings have to be temporary, gearing facilities are not practicable; also, most of the investments that UCITS are permitted to make are liquid. However, liquidity facilities have been used to provide money to fund redemptions where the UCITS did not want to be forced to liquidate certain of its assets to finance those redemptions.

Non-UCITS

The borrowing restrictions applicable to non-UCITS funds depend on who the target investors are. Generally, borrowings may not exceed 25 per cent of the net asset value of the fund. The prospectus of the fund must disclose the fact that the fund intends to engage in leverage.

The Financial Regulator may, on request, disapply the 25 per cent borrowing restriction if the fund is being marketed as a professional investors fund (a PIF). To qualify as a PIF, the fund must have a minimum initial subscription requirement of €125,000 or its equivalent in other currencies and must be marketed to professional investors. In practice, if the minimum initial subscription requirement is satisfied, that is all that is required. The Financial Regulator will generally allow a PIF to leverage 100 per cent of its net assets value although there are examples of permissions being given to engage in leverage of up to 200 per cent of its net asset value.

The Financial Regulator automatically disapplies the borrowing restriction of 25 per cent if the fund is established as a qualifying investor fund (or QIF). For a fund to qualify as a QIF, it must have a minimum initial subscription requirement of €250,000 (or its equivalent in other currencies) and sell its interests to qualifying investors. Qualifying investors are natural persons with a minimum net worth (excluding main residence and household goods) of at least €1.25 million (or its equivalent in other currencies) or any institution that owns or invests on a discretionary basis at least €25 million (or its equivalent in other currencies) or the beneficial owners of which are qualifying investors in their own right. With no regulation-imposed borrowing restriction, leverage is potentially unlimited.

Table 1 summarises the main investment restrictions imposed by the Financial Regulator by fund target investor type.

Table 1: Regulatory investment restrictions (non-UCITS)		
Retail	PIF	QIF
No more than 10% in securities not listed or traded on Financial Regulator approved markets	Generally, the investment restrictions for retail funds will apply but application can be made to the Financial Regulator to disapply one or some of them in whole or in part	Prohibition on acquiring securities with voting rights enabling it to exercise significant influence over the management of the issuer
No more than 10% in securities from a single issuer (with certain limited exceptions)		Except for the above, investment restrictions will not be imposed by the Financial Regulator.
No more than 20% in other regulated investment funds (with limited exceptions)	The Financial Regulator will invariably impose some investment restrictions	However, where the fund is established using a VCC, it must maintain the aim of spreading investment risk as required by the Companies Act 1990
No more than 10% in any class of security issued by a single issuer (with limited exceptions)		
Prohibition on engaging in short selling (selling securities it does not own)		
Prohibition on acquiring securities with voting rights enabling it to exercise significant influence over the management of the issuer		

Lenders will usually seek to impose some form of additional eligibility criteria to the pool of investments made by the fund to determine to what extent they will lend against them and what value they will attribute to that pool of investments. Detailed country, industry sector and individual issuer concentration limits are commonplace, as are provisions determining to what extent the amount paid by the fund for the particular asset will be the amount that the lender will attribute to it. These factors will depend on the nature of the investments the fund is looking to make and they help to highlight one of the areas of tension between lenders and borrowers: the investment manager/sponsor's legitimate concerns about not having the eligibility criteria for the debt financing driving the investment policy of the fund on the one hand and the lender being satisfied with the portfolio of investments.

Source: International Financial Law Review.

How much is invested in the various funds?

This is an interesting question. The following statistics tell part of the story.

SUMMARY OF FUND OF FUNDS UNIT TRUST/OEIC SALES 1996-2006

PERIOD	GROSS SALES £mn					GROSS SALES %				NET SALES £mn				
	Total	Invested internally	Invested externally	Retail	Institutional	Invested internally	Invested externally	Retail	Institutional	Total	Invested internally	Invested externally	Retail	Institutional
1996	872.4	645.1	227.3	738.6	133.8	73.9%	26.1%	84.7%	15.3%	542.5	393.4	149.1	455.0	87.5
1997	1,028.9	797.1	231.8	956.4	72.5	77.5%	22.5%	93.0%	7.0%	582.9	469.2	113.7	576.4	6.5
1998	1,495.3	1,137.4	357.9	1,324.3	171.0	76.1%	23.9%	88.6%	11.4%	712.2	560.3	151.9	711.6	0.6
1999	1,878.8	1,336.6	542.2	1,590.3	288.4	71.1%	28.9%	84.6%	15.4%	991.1	659.8	331.2	786.9	204.2
2000	2,725.2	1,732.6	992.6	2,228.2	496.9	63.6%	36.4%	81.8%	18.2%	1,589.8	872.4	717.5	1,288.8	301.1
2001	2,192.7	1,247.2	945.5	1,722.9	469.8	56.9%	43.1%	78.6%	21.4%	1,042.9	417.6	625.4	732.4	310.6
2002	1,942.6	1,033.1	909.5	1,511.1	431.5	53.2%	46.8%	77.8%	22.2%	834.1	357.0	477.2	542.9	291.3
2003	1,846.1	896.3	949.8	1,309.5	536.7	48.5%	51.5%	70.9%	29.1%	726.7	318.8	407.9	340.4	386.3
2004	3,379.1	1,084.0	2,295.1	2,776.7	602.4	32.1%	67.9%	82.2%	17.8%	1,713.9	184.3	1,529.6	1,361.2	352.7
2005	5,833.8	2,217.2	3,616.6	4,482.8	1,351.0	38.0%	62.0%	76.8%	23.2%	3,249.0	981.7	2,267.3	2,568.5	680.5
2004 Q4	805.6	305.3	500.4	715.8	89.8	37.9%	62.1%	88.9%	11.1%	395.2	86.4	309.8	371.6	24.5
2005 Q1	1,172.9	330.0	842.9	845.6	327.4	28.1%	71.9%	72.1%	27.9%	446.9	88.7	358.2	446.9	0.0
Q2	1,568.5	562.5	996.0	1,328.3	240.2	37.1%	62.9%	84.7%	15.3%	923.8	229.6	694.1	851.7	71.9
Q3	1,331.8	436.3	895.5	1,127.6	204.2	32.8%	67.2%	84.7%	15.3%	744.4	135.5	608.9	616.5	127.9
Q4	1,760.6	868.4	892.2	1,181.4	579.2	49.3%	50.7%	67.1%	32.9%	1,134.1	528.0	606.1	653.4	480.7
2006 Q1	1,843.1	730.4	1,112.7	1,511.7	331.4	39.6%	60.4%	82.0%	18.0%	937.8	402.3	535.5	905.4	32.4
Q2	2,134.7	901.7	1,233.0	1,696.7	438.0	42.2%	57.8%	79.5%	20.5%	1,189.8	485.8	704.0	904.6	285.2
Q3	1,725.1	776.8	948.3	1,244.0	481.1	45.0%	55.0%	72.1%	27.9%	851.2	411.5	439.7	567.8	283.4
2005 Sep	545.0	187.8	357.2	449.2	95.8	34.5%	65.5%	82.4%	17.6%	323.8	63.5	260.2	250.7	73.1
Oct	715.6	378.5	337.0	390.5	325.0	52.9%	47.1%	54.6%	45.4%	486.4	249.1	237.3	191.0	295.3
Nov	525.6	264.6	261.0	382.0	143.6	50.3%	49.7%	72.7%	27.3%	328.0	163.3	164.7	221.5	106.4
Dec	519.4	225.3	294.2	408.8	110.6	43.4%	56.6%	78.7%	21.3%	319.8	115.7	204.1	240.9	78.9
2006 Jan	497.7	191.9	305.8	398.5	99.3	38.6%	61.4%	80.1%	19.9%	293.8	98.5	195.4	238.2	55.8
Feb	515.2	209.7	305.5	424.9	90.3	40.7%	59.3%	82.5%	17.5%	283.5	103.8	179.7	229.1	54.4
Mar	830.1	328.8	501.3	688.3	141.8	39.6%	60.4%	82.9%	17.1%	360.5	200.1	160.4	438.1	-77.6
Apr	831.3	339.6	491.5	725.5	105.8	40.9%	59.1%	87.3%	12.7%	533.2	236.4	296.8	461.3	71.9
May	651.5	254.4	397.2	515.3	136.2	39.0%	61.0%	79.1%	20.9%	307.6	82.2	225.3	231.2	76.4
Jun	651.9	307.5	344.4	455.8	196.1	47.2%	52.8%	69.9%	30.1%	349.1	167.3	181.8	212.2	136.9
Jul	579.7	275.9	303.8	412.9	166.8	47.6%	52.4%	71.2%	28.8%	277.7	172.9	104.8	214.4	63.3
Aug	602.3	264.0	338.3	423.1	179.2	43.8%	56.2%	70.3%	29.7%	359.0	149.0	210.0	205.7	153.3
Sep	543.1	236.9	306.2	408.0	135.2	43.6%	56.4%	75.1%	24.9%	214.5	89.6	124.9	147.7	66.8

Note - Each month small revisions to figures may have been made since previous press release. This reflects additional information received.

"Invested internally" and "Invested externally" distinguishes between fund of funds invested solely "internally" as opposed to both "internally" and "externally" of the group.

In fund of funds those investing "internally" may alternatively use the terms investing in "own" or "fettered". Likewise those investing in "other" or "unfettered".

Equity includes the following sectors: UK All Companies, UK Smaller Companies, UK Equity Income, Japan, Japanese Smaller Companies, UK Equity & Bond Income, North America, North American Smaller Companies, Asia Pacific Including Japan, Asia Pacific Excluding Japan,

Europe Including UK, Europe Excluding UK, Cit, UK Index Linked Gilts, UK Corporate Bond, UK Other Bond, UK Zeros and Global Bond.

Bond includes the following sectors: UK Gilt, UK Index Linked Gilts, UK Corporate Bond, UK Other Bond, UK Zeros and Global Bond.

Money Market includes the following sector: Money Market

Balanced includes the following sectors: Active Managed, Balanced Managed, Cautious Managed and UK Equity & Bond Income.

Other includes the following sectors: Guaranteed/Protected Funds, Pensions and Unclassified Sector. Note - Each month small revisions to figures may have been made since previous press release. This reflects additional information received.

Fund of funds are not counted towards the sector total.

"Invested internally" and "Invested externally" distinguishes between fund of funds invested solely "internally" as opposed to "externally" and externally"of the group.

In fund of funds those investing internally may alternatively use the terms investing in "own" or "fettered". Likewise those investing internally and externally may use the terms investing in "other" or "unfettered".

Source : IMA ; www.investmentuk.org/statistics/qtrly/2006/q309.pdf

Products and assets used in portfolio management

Not surprisingly today there is a very wide range of products from different areas of the capital markets that fund managers use in their strategies.

Figure 1.3 shows just some of those products at high level and also shows that with something like derivatives, these may be held in a portfolio as a position in its own right or as a position related to another asset class like equity for instance.

The type of products used obviously has an impact on the administrator's work. Many of the "vanilla" products are not of significant issue to the administrator but clearly the more "exotic" ones are. We need to be aware that when we talk about products like derivatives we do have a major difference between the exchange-traded products like futures and options and the products traded over the counter. Prices for exchange-traded products are easily obtainable and most exchange-traded products are likely to be acceptable in terms of regulation, etc. There will be margin calls for futures and written option positions and as a result collateral in the form of cash or assets will need to be provided. This will mainly be an issue for the custodian but the fund records and accounting for the products and collateral will need to be correct.

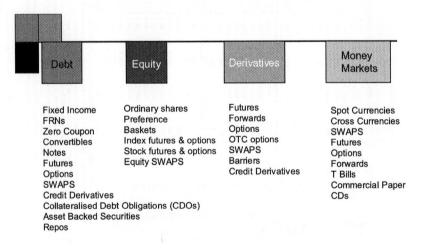

Figure 1.3 Capital Markets

2

Hedge funds

Hedge funds are not new. They were first established some 40 or so years ago; so whilst hedge funds are not particularly new, the growth of hedge funds into a $600 billion plus market has happened relatively recently.

The first hedge fund started in 1949. The simple idea of looking to profit in falling as well as rising markets was supplemented by the idea that the fund manager should be rewarded for their skill and expertise in providing growth for the investor. These same principles drive the expansion of the hedge fund industry that continues today.

To find a definition for hedge funds is not easy. In reality the hedge fund industry, like all markets, is divided into sectors covering strategies. These, we can say, cover areas of investment like:

- Global Asset Allocation
- Relative Value
- Event-driven
- Equity Hedge
- Short-selling.

A manager using any of these strategies has a very different objective and as a result employs different strategies and investments in the course of management of the funds it has under management.

We can take a brief look at the types of strategies and investment each of the sectors would typically be involved in. In general terms a hedge fund has a much wider brief than say a mutual fund and can therefore look at situations, markets, products, etc to employ in strategies that would not be available to other managers.

Market neutral (or relative value) funds

Market neutral funds attempt to produce returns that have no or low correlation with traditional markets such as the UK, European, Japanese and US equity or fixed income markets. Market neutral strategies are characterised less by what they invest in than by the nature of the returns. They often are highly quantitative in their portfolio construction process, and market themselves as an investment that can improve the overall risk/return structure of a portfolio of investments. Market neutral funds should not be confused with Long/Short investment strategies (see below). The key feature of market neutral funds is the low correlation between their returns and that of the traditional assets.

Long/short funds

Funds employing long/short strategies generally invest in equity and fixed income securities taking directional bets on either an individual security, sector or even country level. For example, a fund might do pairs trading, and buy stocks that they think will move up and sell stocks they think will move down. Or go long of the sectors they think will go up and short countries they think will go down often using derivatives like index futures. Long/Short strategies are not automatically market neutral. That is, a long/short strategy can have significant correlation with traditional markets.

Tactical trading

Tactical trading refers to strategies that speculate on the direction of market prices of currencies, commodities, equities and/or bonds. Managers typically are either systematic or discretionary. Systematic managers are primarily trend followers who rely on computer models based on technical analysis. Discretionary managers usually take a less quantitative approach and rely on both fundamental and technical analysis. This is the most volatile sector in terms of performance because many managers combine long and/or short positions with leverage to maximise the potential returns.

Global asset allocation funds

They can invest in a wide range of markets and investments including private equity in emerging markets. They involve leveraging positions using derivatives and will change exposures to take advantage of the global market movements.

Event-driven funds

Invests in situations that will respond to events, possibly takeovers and entities benefiting from the outcome of events like wars, political change, environmental issues, etc., as well as general economic events like currency fluctuations. Such events also include distressed debt investing, merger arbitrage which is sometimes called risk arbitrage, and corporate spin-offs and restructuring.

Short-selling funds

These are funds that are seeking to profit from falls in value of investments, markets, etc. and do so by holding short positions that are often heavily geared. They are likely to have some long positions as they will need to provide collateral for the stock borrowing needed against the short positions. In that sense they are not unlike the long/short funds described above.

Arbitrage funds

Other types of hedge funds are structured to profit from arbitrage possibilities and these include the likes of

- Fixed income arbitrage
- Convertible bond arbitrage
- Mortgage-backed security arbitrage
- Derivatives arbitrage.

In addition we have Funds of Hedge Funds which are designed to provide investors with a vehicle that enables a broad exposure to different hedge funds in exactly the same way as a unit trust or indeed a fund of funds trust does.

It is important to reiterate that, despite the common assumptions that are made, not all hedge funds are massively risky, highly geared products. However, from a regulatory point of view, the sale of hedge funds has been restricted to high net worth clients; for example those with at least $1 million of assets and an income of $300,000*.

A fund of funds is offered to investors with lower net worth on the basis that the risk is diversified through this type of vehicle (see Figure 2.1).

We also need to be aware that in the hedge fund world there are Master Feeder Funds. These are quite different from a fund of funds.

A master feeder is a fund that manages the investment for more than one hedge fund simultaneously. Typically this is where the same

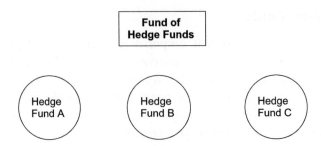

Figure 2.1   Fund of Hedge Funds

manager established two funds aimed at different groups of investors, perhaps for tax and/or domicile reasons. The investment is made through the single master feeder fund and is then distributed to the sub-funds.

How are hedge funds structured?

There are several phases in the establishing of a hedge fund.

The initial consideration is naturally what type of fund will it be?

All funds not just hedge funds are either closed or open-ended funds, i.e. they have a fluctuating number of shares in issue or they have a fixed number of shares in issue. Then there is the question of what objectives and strategies the fund will have. Is it focused on a domestic market or international markets or both and also where are its clients likely to be domiciled?

These are questions for the fund owners and/or manager and once decided upon there are then the various areas of the infrastructure of the support for the fund and its investment activity which need to be considered. Broadly speaking these are as follows:

1. Legally establishing the fund
2. Regulatory Issues
3. Marketing (for a retail fund)
4. Finance and Administrative Support (Fund Administration)
    a.   Banking
    b.   Trading
    c.   Custody
    d.   Reporting
    e.   Valuations
    f.   Registration/Transfer Agency
    g.   Performance Management
    h.   Compliance.

The main relationships are often those between the manager, the prime broker and the fund administrator. This leaves the manager free to concentrate on the investment policies and transactions. It can also be important to have expert advice on various issues, particularly the legal and tax matters that will affect the fund.

For instance applying for the registration of the fund and establishing the tax situation in respect of the investors is crucial to the overall success of the fund.

Properly structuring a hedge fund product for the market is critically important and will be a major determining factor in its overall success. In structuring an onshore or offshore hedge fund, there are several key areas that must be evaluated.

Addressing these areas prior to starting up a fund (or funds) can eliminate a multitude of problems later on and is a reason why very often the promoters of a hedge fund will seek the assistance of the fund administrator in the set-up phase.

It is important to understand that all of these areas are closely related and can easily impact on one or more areas, so whilst different parties could be involved, centralising the process via the fund administrator can have significant benefits.

Hedge funds can take many forms but we can assume that the typical hedge fund manager is looking to create fund products for high net worth and institutional investors. The major distinction here being that these are not to be retail, publicly offered products, which would be subject to more stringent regulatory requirements. This is a very generic overview of the issues in setting up a fund and there are likely to be other issues that must be evaluated when putting together a specific fund.

Tax issues

The tax issues to be evaluated can relate to three clear areas: (1) the type of the investors; (2) the investment manager(s); and (3) the investment strategy/programme.

Investors in different parts of the world will, naturally, have differing preferences as to how the hedge fund is structured. For instance in the US taxpayers generally prefer to be in domestically organised vehicles that are a flow-through entity for tax purposes, such as a limited partnership. In a flow-through entity, the entity itself pays no taxes, but rather the profits "flow through" to the investors who are responsible for paying any taxes due.

US tax-exempt investors, including ERISA money, will generally prefer to invest directly into an offshore entity that is not a flow through, such as a corporation. The reason they prefer this is that were they to invest in a flow-through vehicle, they may be subject to taxes on any gains relating to leverage, which for US tax purposes would include short sales, a common strategy of hedge fund managers.

Offshore investors will in most cases prefer to invest into an offshore fund company.

As far as the tax implications for the fund manager is concerned, the manager will more than likely want to ensure that the offshore fund has provisions to allow deferral of management and incentive fees. This will allow the manager to defer his or her fees for a predetermined period and allow them to grow along with the fund on a tax-deferred basis. It is important to understand that the election to defer has nothing to do with the fact that the entity is offshore, but rather that it is not a flow-through vehicle. Were it a flow-through vehicle, the fees would not be reflected as expenses for tax purposes and the investors would be paying tax on profits associated with these fees (particularly incentive fees). Deferral of compensation is a standard tool in compensation plans in the United States and can be particularly valuable to implement in the context of an offshore fund.

The tax situation for funds and investors in other jurisdictions can vary from those that apply in the case of US investors and funds, and we cannot cover all eventualities in this book although some further details can be found on the websites of the funds management companies (also tax situations change constantly so it is imperative for the fund administrator to have up-to-date information on this through their own tax expert or an external tax expert as appropriate).

Regulatory issues

As far as the regulatory position is concerned, there may be a big difference if it is planned that the product will be sold to US investors. When US investors are involved, the manager will rely upon an exemption under Regulation D, which allows for the sale of private placements to sophisticated investors, but the manager must bear in mind that he or she cannot publicly solicit or advertise the product in any way.

If the fund will be trading in derivatives like futures and if it has US investors, it will need to register with the Commodity Futures Trading Commission (CFTC) and the manager will need to register as an xxxxx (CPO) or an xxxxx (CTA). In general, hedge funds rely upon exemptions under CFTC Rule 4.7, which limits the fund to qualified eligible participants. Use of this exemption will significantly reduce the disclosure and reporting requirements the fund administrator will need to produce for the manager and the fund to an administratively manageable level.

Stock exchange listings should be evaluated for offshore products. Amongst the exchanges that are used for listings we find:

- Irish Stock Exchange
- Bermuda
- Channel Isles
- Cayman
- Luxembourg
- British Virgin Isles
- Isle of Man.

There are other exchanges on which a fund can be listed but the main reason for listing is to allow institutional investors to include the products in their portfolios and as these institutional funds are very important source of investors for many hedge funds a listing becomes imperative.

It is worth noting here how the financial centre in Dublin has grown enormously on the back of hedge funds listing on the exchange.

Business issues

Among the many business issues that arise, it is particularly important for fund administrators to focus on those that relate to:

- Risk management
- Calculation of the NAV in accordance with the terms of the fund and/or regulation
- Publication of the price of the shares/units in accordance with the terms of the fund and/or regulation
- Calculation and payment of the correct incentive fees to the manager
- Maintenance of the accounting records and preparation of the accounts in accordance with the regulatory requirements and accounting standards
- Ensuring compliance by the fund and fund manager
- Ensuring the suitability and qualification of investors in the fund

On the fee side, it is crucial to understand that there is an inherent flaw in the calculation of incentive fees for corporate entities. For instance the fund that is a partnership will have capital accounts for each partner and, therefore, the fee can be readily determined by the profits associated with each account. In contrast, a company has shares that will have the same price per share, including an accrual for the incentive fee. Since investors buy their shares at different times and, consequently, different prices, one may have a profit while the other has a loss. Therefore, we could have one investor with an incentive fee and the other without, which implies two different share prices. Under this scenario the manager may not earn all the fees he or she should, and there may be some subsidising between investors. Some form of equalisation of the situation is required and there are methodologies that correct these anomalies, which managers and administrators should explore and which are covered later in the book.

Investment issues

The investment strategy must be evaluated within the context of the fund structure. Some adjustments to the asset allocation within the fund will be needed from time to time and will usually relate to one or more of investment opportunities, subscriptions/redemptions, tax and regulatory issues.

In some situations the influence of the prime broker may determine investment issues particularly in terms of loans, collateral, exposures, gearing, etc.

Marketing issues

There are many issues that need to be evaluated to ensure that the final fund product that is offered is an attractive one. The most common are liquidity (how easy is it to buy and sell shares in the fund or is there some kind of restriction that means the investment must be held for a certain period of time), valuation frequency, fee structures, jurisdictional selection, regulatory issues like registrations and reporting and investment guidelines or restrictions. The products must be tailored to meet the needs of the target investors. For example, if the manager would like to attract investment from the manager of a fund of funds group, they will need to be offering good liquidity and probably daily NAV calculation. In addition, offshore investors generally prefer share-based entities, i.e. companies as opposed to limited partnerships.

The fund administrator may wish to ensure that the manager has, in the fund documentation, provided flexibility in terms of incentivising third-party marketing groups and allowed for special fee arrangements for lead institutional or substantial investors. It is also during the structuring stage that the manager, with the help and advice of the administrator, will want to evaluate where prices will be published, where to list the fund, and to which databases to provide performance. It is most important to recognise that the provision of this information must be carefully monitored to ensure compliance with applicable regulatory requirements.

Operational issues

It is very important to ensure that the final product will be manageable from an operational standpoint. The key concept here is to "keep it simple". Failure to do so will usually result in internal and external confusion; increased operational, audit and legal expenses; delays in reporting valuations to investors; and, delays in preparation of year-end tax reporting. This could easily lead to loss of clients and/or unwelcome regulatory/tax issues.

In addition, and depending upon the complexity of the overall structure, there may be accounting issues to be examined as well as pricing issues and the formulation of the pricing policy.

Another important area that the manager and administrator will also want to consider is the pros and cons of using a master-feeder structure as opposed to stand-alone funds for onshore and offshore investors. Essentially, a master-feeder has two feeders – one for onshore investors and one for offshore investors – whose sole investment is an interest in a third company, the master, which contains a single investment portfolio. The advantages of this structure are

- A single portfolio (no trades to allocate and only on reconciliation)
- Uniform track record
- Creation of critical mass
- The ability to create additional private-label products quickly and efficiently with a fully diversified and invested portfolio.

Many hedge fund managers would like to manage money for both US and non-US investors. When this is the case the manager will probably look to create a domestic US limited partnership for the US investors, and an offshore fund for the non-US investors. This will meet the potential tax requirements for each of these groups. However by doing so, there are certain basic inefficiencies created, the most obvious one being that the manager now has two quite separate portfolios to manage. This will result in a requirement to allocate trades amongst these portfolios and the need to try to maintain similar performance between the two portfolios. This is time-consuming and creates more administrative costs.

This is where the structure commonly referred to as "master feeder" can resolve these inefficiencies. The application of this structure to hedge fund groups (and indeed others) can help both the manager and investors. A master-feeder structure is comprised of three entities: one "master" company and two "feeders". Under this scenario the feeders would probably be set up as a limited partnership organised in the US for US investors and an offshore company for non-US investors. The sole investment of these two feeders would be an ownership interest in the third entity – the master. It is at the master company level that the actual portfolio of investments would be made and managed, thus consolidating all the trading activities into a single portfolio. This master company would typically be an offshore entity and be organised as a limited liability company to preserve the tax treatment of both US and non-US investors.

Defining responsibilities

It is important that all parties know their role and whilst each hedge fund is unique some generic requirements and responsibilities can be established:

1. The investment manager will have responsibility for the strategy implementation, asset allocation and meeting the return objectives.
2. The custodian will hold the assets of the fund in electronic or physical format.
3. The prime broker will provide market access, financing, securities lending and possibly the custody and marketing capabilities.
4. The fund administrator may be involved in the set-up, marketing of the fund and also ensuring the manager is complying with the fund's terms and objectives, valuation, fund accounting and the transfer agency role. For example:
   a. Compile an Administration Agreement to act as the terms of the relationship between the fund and the administrator.
   b. Provide secretarial services such as the preparation of resolutions for the opening of bank and brokerage accounts (could be done by the legal counsel).
   c. Prepare resolutions for any additional accounts required.
   d. Provide guidance concerning jurisdiction selection and relevant regulatory issues.
   e. Determine the structure of entities related to the fund.
   f. Review all offering and legal documents.
   g. Make arrangements for legal, banking, brokerage and audit services for the fund.
   h. Assistance in location and selection/provision of offshore directors.
   i. Serve as coordinator and link between the manager and all relevant parties including providing investor services (the role of the transfer agency is covered in more detail later in the book).

Fund set-up summary

Obviously there are many interrelated issues that must be considered when putting hedge fund products together. They encompass a broad range of investment styles, strategies and assets, the final structure affecting the success of the end product. It is also important to understand that these types of issues will vary from one manager to the next as no two hedge funds are likely to be exactly the same. Managers and fund administrators are going to be very closely involved in the set-up and then running of the fund; however it will ultimately be the fund's legal counsel that must compile the legal documents and sign off on the structure.

We can deduce from the above that the fund administrators must be diligent and efficient in the service they provide, otherwise between them the manager and administrator will increase the cost of the project, cause delays in launching, and possibly have an end result of a flawed or inferior product.

3

Mutual funds and OEICs

Background

Mutual funds and Open Ended Investment Companies (OEICs), some-times called Investment Companies with Variable Capital (ICVCs), are collective investment schemes.

According to some sources in the industry like the excellent Investo-pedia, historians are uncertain of the origins of investment funds. Some cite the closed-end investment companies launched in the Netherlands in 1822 by King William I as the first mutual funds while others point to a Dutch merchant named Adriaan van Ketwich whose investment trust created in 1774 may have given the king the idea. Van Ketwich probably theorised that diversification would increase the appeal of investments to smaller investors with minimal capital. The name of van Ketwich's fund, *Eendragt Maakt Magt*, translates to "unity creates strength". The next wave of near-mutual funds included an investment trust launched in Switzerland in 1849, followed by similar vehicles created in Scotland in the 1880s. The idea of pooling resources and spreading risk using closed-end investments soon took root in Great Britain and France, making its way to the United States in the 1890s.

Open-ended funds appeared in the 1920s and today there are copious numbers of funds that relate to different markets, sectors and assets.

In the UK unit trusts were by far the most popular pooled investment but the introduction of regulation permitting OEICs has led to some unit trusts converting to investment companies.

OEICs

The structure of an OEIC is based around the authorised corporate director, the owner/issuer and the depositary who monitors the activity of the fund to ensure its compliance with the prospectus.

The OEIC can issue registered shares or bearer shares or indeed both. The share register of the OEIC must be updated daily and include the registered and bearer share holdings of the ACD and the registered share holdings of the investors.

The issue, sale, redemption or cancellation price of a share will be at a single mid-market price – "single pricing" – and that price will be the net asset value which reflects the market value of the OEICs investments. Shares must be issued or redeemed at net asset value on each dealing day when dealings take place.

Dilution levy

The actual costs of purchasing or selling the shares may be higher than the value used in calculating the share price. Under certain circumstances, e.g. large deals, this may have an adverse effect on the shareholders' interest in the fund. In order to prevent this effect – dilution – the ACD has the power to require the payment by share-holders of a dilution levy either as an addition to the issue price of shares or as a deduction from the cancellation price. The ACD must pay the dilution levy, if charged, to the OEIC where it becomes part of the scheme property.

Share classes

The shares in an OEIC may consist of a number of different classes, as listed below.

Income shares

These are shares that have income allocated periodically to the share-holders. The amount of any income distribution is paid to shareholders in accordance with the terms of the fund.

Net accumulation shares

These are shares in respect of which income (net of tax deducted by the company) is credited periodically to capital. The income distribution is not paid out to the shareholder but added to the capital of the OEIC and so is reinvested.

Gross accumulation shares

These are shares where income is credited periodically to capital but, in accordance with relevant tax law, without deduction of any income tax by the company.

Currency class shares

An OEIC will have a base currency, which is specified in the instrument of incorporation, and is the currency in which the accounts of the OEIC are prepared. However, an OEIC is able to issue shares in different currencies. Where currency class shares are issued, such shares must be in a different currency to the base currency of the OEIC and the prices of the shares and distributions must be expressed in the same currency as the shares. Statements and certificates of amounts of money or value must also be given in the same currency as the shares and conversions from the base currency is to be at a rate of exchange that does not materially prejudice the interest of shareholders.

Currency class income shares in respect of which income is allocated periodically to share holders, currency class net accumulation shares in respect of which income is credited periodically to capital and currency class gross accumulation shares in respect of which income is credited periodically to capital, but in accordance with relevant tax law, without deduction of any income tax by the company.

Different rights

An OEIC may not issue a class of share in which the rights to participate in the capital property, income property or distributions are different to the rights of any other share class or where payments or accumulation of income or capital would differ in source or form from those of any other class. This means, for example, that the "split-capital" structure, which is a common feature of investment trust companies, cannot be used by an OEIC.

Share classes may, however, have different rights to reflect accumulation of income rather than distribution, different charging structures (this relates to different charges and expenses that may be taken from the scheme property or payable by the shareholder) or currencies.

The role of the depositary

The depositary makes sure that the OEIC is managed in accordance with the regulations and the prospectus of the fund.

The role of the custodian

The custodian holds the assets of the fund separately from the investment manager. They also manage the assets in terms of areas like for instance income collection, withholding tax, etc.

Regulation determines this and the fund administrator will need to be aware of the various EU and US directives and regulation, for example the Section 17(f) of the Investment Company Act in the US and the Client Asset and Client Money Rules in the UK and Europe.

Advantages over unit trusts

Open Ended Investment Companies have some advantages over unit trusts, including being able to be marketed more easily and to a wider audience, they have a less complex legal structure than a trust as they are formed under Company rather than Trust Law.

Another advantage is that any initial charge is shown as a separate item on the investors' transaction statement. By contrast, the charges for a unit trust are included in the buying and selling prices, which makes it more difficult for the investor to understand the real costs they are incurring.

Another major advantage is the ability to establish a single umbrella OEIC that has a series of funds within it specialising in particular areas. These are known as sub-funds and allow investors' money to be put to work in specialist areas such as UK equity or emerging markets – the choice is vast.

Hedge vs mutual funds: A comparison

Hedge fund mangers do not just focus on beating an index – they aim to deliver positive or absolute returns regardless of market direction. Under absolute return investing, the manager has the flexibility to use advanced investment strategies to maximise returns, without the constraint of managing to a benchmark.

Hedge funds	Mutual funds
• 'Absolute' return objective	• 'Relative' return objective
• Flexible investment strategies	• Limited investment strategies
• Unconstrained by benchmark index	• Constrained by a benchmark index
• Lower correlation to markets	• Higher correlation to markets
• Take long and short positions	• Take long-only positions
• May employ leverage	• No use of leverage
• Manager fees tied to performance	• Manager fees not typically tied to performance
• Usually large minimum investment size	• Small minimum investment size
• Usually sold by Offering Memorandum only	• Usually sold by Prospectus only

Source: Bluemont Capital.

4

Private equity

Private equity essentially is the investment in shares of a company that are not normally listed or tradable.

These types of companies rely on being able to raise finance by attracting particular kinds of investors mainly because whilst there is scope for significant return if the company grows and is successful, there is equally a risk that the firm may fail and most or probably all of the investment lost.

Generally speaking, private equity funds are organised as limited partnerships which are controlled by the private equity firm that acts as the general partner. The fund obtains commitments from certain qualified investors such as pension funds, financial institutions and wealthy individuals to invest a specified amount. These investors become passive or what is referred to as limited partners, i.e. they have no involvement in the direct decision-making but instead their involvement in the fund partnership is such that at the time the general partner identifies an appropriate investment opportunity, it is entitled to "call" the required equity capital. At this time each limited partner funds a pro rata portion of this commitment. All investment decisions are made by the General Partner that also manages the fund's investments, i.e. the portfolio. Over the life of a fund which often extends up to 10 years, the fund will typically make between 15 and 25 separate investments with for instance no single investment exceeding 10 per cent of the total commitments. This helps to reduce the risk of a total loss of investment.

General partners, as with other fund managers, are typically compensated with a management fee, defined as a percentage of the fund's total equity capital, as well as a carried interest (see below), defined as a percentage of profits generated by the fund (so long as some minimum return for the investors called the hurdle rate is achieved).

For example, the general partner of funds might receive a management fee of 2 per cent and carried interest of 20 per cent. The carry may be reduced by the amount of fees received over a period.

Gross private equity returns may be in excess of 20 per cent per year, which in the case of leveraged buyout firms is primarily due to the ability to gain exposure via borrowing and, in the case of venture capital firms, due to the high level of risk associated with early stage investments.

A leveraged buyout (LBO), sometimes referred to as highly leveraged transaction (HLT) or 'bootstrap' transaction, occurs when a financial sponsor gains control of a majority of a target company's issued shares through the use of borrowed money or debt.

An LBO is essentially a strategy involving the acquisition of another company using a significant amount of borrowed money (bonds or loans) to meet the cost of acquisition. Often, the assets of the company being acquired are used as collateral for the loans in addition to the assets of the acquiring company. The purpose of LBO is to allow companies to make large acquisitions without having to commit a lot of capital. In an LBO, it is not unusual for there to be a ratio of 70 per cent debt to 30 per cent equity.

Definition of carried interest

It is the portion of any gains realised by the fund to which the fund managers are entitled, generally without having to contribute capital to the fund. Carried interest payments are customary in the venture capital industry, in order to create a significant economic incentive for venture capital fund managers to achieve capital gains.

Nearly $180 billion of private equity was invested globally in 2004, up over a half on the previous year as market confidence and trading conditions improved. Funds raised globally increased 40 per cent in 2004 to $112 billion. Prior to this, investments and funds raised increased markedly during the 1990s to reach record levels in 2000. The subsequent falls in 2001 and 2002 were due to the slowdown in the global economy and declines in equity markets, particularly in the technology sector. The decline in fund-raising between 2000 and 2003 was also due to a large overhang created by the end of 2000 between funds raised and funds invested.

The regional breakdown of private equity activity shows that in 2004, 66 per cent of global private equity investments (up from 58 per cent in 1998) and 62 per cent of funds raised (down from 72 per cent) were managed in North America. Between 1998 and 2004, Europe increased its share of investments (from 24 to 26 per cent) and funds raised (from 18 to 31 per cent). Asia-Pacific region's share of investments and of funds raised during this period was virtually unchanged around 6 per cent while share of the rest of the world fell. The country breakdown for private equity activity shows that private equity firms in the US managed 64 per cent of global investments and 59 per cent of funds raised in 2004. The UK was the second largest private equity centre with 13 per cent of investments and 11 per cent of funds raised (*Source*: Wikipedia).

Venture capital funds

Venture capital general partners (also known as 'venture capitalists' or 'VCs') may be former senior managers at firms similar to those which the partnership funds. Investors in venture capital funds are limited partners and are typically large institutions with large amounts of available capital, such as pension funds, insurance companies and pooled investment vehicles. Some other terms associated with positions in venture capital firms include venture partners and entrepreneur-in-residence (EIR). Venture partners 'bring in deals' and receive income only on deals they work on as opposed to general partners who receive income on all deals.

EIRs are experts in a particular domain and bring their experience into performing due diligence on potential deals. EIRs are usually engaged by VC firms temporarily, say up to 18 months, and are expected to develop and offer ideas.

Amongst the many variations of private equity and in particular venture funds are fixed-lifetime funds.

Indeed many venture capital funds have a fixed life of 10 years. This model was pioneered by some of the most successful funds through the 1980s when technology start-ups in particular were seeking funding. The concept was to invest in technological trends broadly but only during their period of ascendance and not to maintain that exposure to the management and marketing risks of any individual firm or its product.

In such a fund, the investors have a fixed commitment to the fund that is 'called down' by the VCs over time as the fund makes its investments. In a typical venture capital fund, the VCs receive an annual management fee equal to 2 per cent of the committed capital to the fund and 20 per cent of the net profits of the fund ("2 and 20").

It is worth noting that because a fund may run out of capital prior to the end of its life, the larger VCs usually have several overlapping funds at the same time. Timing of the fund getting out of the firms it invests in is obviously crucially important.

Venture capital funds often use common enough products in their portfolio, for instance, preferred shares, ordinary shares or a combination of equity and debt issues like, for example, convertible bonds. These convertible bonds may be structured so that if a certain level of risk is exceeded they become equity. Most venture capital funds have an exit strategy such as an initial public offering of the company invested in or an acquisition of the company. This can happen over a period of say 3 to 7 years and the equity held by the VC fund enables the fund to do this.

In most cases, one or more general partners of the investing fund joins the Board of the start-up company and will often help to recruit personnel to key management positions.

Venture capital is not suitable for all investors or for that matter companies seeking money. Venture capitalists tend to be very selective in deciding what to invest, in perhaps only one in several hundred opportunities offered to them.

Generally speaking the venture capital fund is most interested in ventures with high growth potential, as only such opportunities are likely to be capable of providing the financial returns and successful exit event within the required timeframe that VCs expect. Because of such expectations, most venture funding goes into companies in the fast-growing sectors of the markets. In the past this has included sectors like for instance, technology.

As noted above VCs hope to be able to sell their shares, warrants, options, convertibles, or other forms of equity within 3 to 7 years, at or after an exit event; this is referred to as harvesting. Venture capitalists know that not all their investments will pay off. The failure rate of investments can be high; anywhere from 20–90 per cent of the enterprises funded fail to return the invested capital.

Many venture capitalists try to mitigate the risk of failure through diversification. They invest in companies in different industries and different countries so that the risk across the portfolio is reduced.

Many concentrate their investments in the industry that they are familiar with. In either case, they usually work on the assumption that for every ten investments they make, two will be failures, two will be successful and six will be marginally successful. They expect that the two successes will pay for the time given, and risk exposure of the other eight. In good times, the funds that do succeed may offer returns of 300–1000 per cent (*Source*: Wikipedia) to investors!!

Whilst venture capital and private equity funds can produce stunning returns it is not always the case. The NASDAQ crash and technology

slump that started in March 2000 for instance and the resulting catas-
trophic losses on overvalued, non-performing start-up firms impacted
massively on VC funds. By 2003 many VCs were focused on writing off
companies they funded just a few years earlier, and many funds were
left worthless than when invested in. Venture capital investors sought
to reduce the large commitments they have made to VC funds.

US firms have traditionally been the biggest participants in venture
deals, but non-US venture investment is growing. Europe has a large
and growing number of active venture firms. Capital raised in the
region in 2005, including buy-out funds, exceeded €60 billion, of which
€12.6 billion was specifically for venture investment.

Estimates of VC funding of companies in India was expected to
reach $1 billion by the end of 2004 (*Source*: Indian Venture Capital
Association), and in China, venture funding more than doubled from
$420 million in 2002 to almost $1 billion in 2003.

Fund administration

Clearly the main issue with both private equity and VC funds is likely to
be getting a realistic value of a start-up company. Daily valuations are
neither practical nor of any real value. Specialist help from accountants
in the area of private company valuation will be needed.

Accounting issues are also important particularly the writing off of
failed investments as well as the correct managing of the carried interest
and management fees. When or if the investments get to the exit strategy
or event then again the correct accounting for the realisation of the
investment is essential for the general partner and investor.

Many private equity and VC funds can attract tax advantages for
investors and the administrator in the fund set-up stage and when
dealing with the investor awareness of the advantages and disadvan-
tages in the tax field is required.

5

Unit trusts

Origins of the unit trust

Unit trusts are not new. They were first established in the United States in the 1930s. Early unit trusts were closed funds and were passive, that is to say the manager had little scope to vary the investments held in the fund.

The first unit trust was launched in the UK in 1931. The rationale behind the launch was to emulate the comparative robustness of US mutual funds through the 1929 Wall Street crash. The first trust called the 'First British Fixed Trust' managed by M&G held the shares of 24 leading companies in a fixed portfolio that was not changed for a fixed lifespan of 20 years. The trust was relaunched as the M&G General Trust and later renamed as the Blue Chip Fund (*Source*: M&G/Wikipedia).

By 1939 there were around 100 trusts in the UK, managing funds in the region of £80 million (*Source*: M&G/Wikipedia).

The unit trusts that are in existence today tend to be actively managed and fall into one of the following categories:

- Securities funds
- Property funds
- Futures and Options Funds
- Geared Futures and Options funds
- Warrant funds
- Money Market funds
- Umbrella funds.

Unit trusts are established under trust rather than company law. As collective investment schemes, investors' subscriptions that purchase units in the trust are invested in accordance with the Scheme Particulars. Most unit trusts these days are open-ended and units in the trust are created and cancelled by the Trustee, an organisation that holds the assets of the trust on behalf of the beneficial owners, i.e. the unit holders who have invested in the trust.

The scheme manager ('fund manager') makes the investment decisions and deals with the investors wishing to buy and sell units. The manager is responsible for valuing the assets in the trust and making the price at which investors can buy or sell.

The published price of the units is controlled and so the manager must establish a creation and redemption price. Once established the manager can publish a dealing price that is no greater than the creation price and not less than the redemption price.

For example:

Creation Price: 128.0550   Redemption Price: 127.5000

The manager can publish the price at which they will deal as 128.00 and 127.75.

Note that the price of the units is made to four significant figures.

Unit trusts in the UK are either authorised unit trusts under the Financial Markets Act 2000 or unauthorised. In the case of unauthorised unit trusts these cannot be sold to the general public.

Buying and selling units

Unit trust units are bought and sold through the fund manager. Their value moves in line with the overall value of the fund, which in turn moves in line with changes to the underlying asset prices in the fund.

Some unit trusts provide for dividend income or interest distributions from the units, based on the dividends or interest paid by the underlying shares or other investments.

Like most investments, there are charges that investors have to pay to cover the expenses of managing funds. These charges can vary considerably.

Charges

Investors usually pay an initial charge when they buy (this charge leads to a difference – called the "spread" – between the prices at which investors can buy and sell units). The initial charge is usually reduced or even eliminated if they buy through a discount broker or Internet fund supermarket.

Some unit trusts have no initial charge – sometimes there is an "exit charge" instead when investors withdraw their money by redeeming units. This is often limited to a period of say five years and the charge falls each year until it reaches zero after the investor has held the units for the required period.

With umbrella funds there is usually no exit/initial charge for switching between funds in the umbrella.

With all unit trusts, the company running it takes a yearly management fee direct from the investment fund.

Investors' lump sum or regular contributions are used by the fund manager to buy a wide range of shares. These shares are pooled together and repackaged as units with a unit price reflecting the value of the investments. The unit price is one way that the trust can build in charges.

Unit prices

Investors can only buy and sell units through the fund manager. As noted above there are usually two different prices:

1. the "*offer*" price – the price you pay to *buy* units, and
2. the "*bid*" price – the price you get for *selling* units.

The difference between the two prices is called the "bid/offer spread" and, according to the UK's Financial Service Authority's Consumer Fact Sheet, it is typically 5–6 per cent in most unit trusts. This means that £1000 invested in units with a bid/offer spread of 5 per cent immediately reduces the value of your investment to £950. The bid/offer spread usually includes an "initial charge". This is an upfront fee received by the fund management company and often paid out to financial advisers. Some unit trusts charge much less than 5 per cent – many "tracker" funds for example.

For the fund administrator there are several key issues with unit trusts.

Clearly there is the charging and recording of the fees plus the calculation of the NAV so that the spread can be published by the manager.

Add to this the calculation of the income and if applicable the distribution of that income to the investors.

The unit trust also publishes Scheme Particulars and Key Features documents for investors. Details of the content can be found on the websites of the funds management companies.

6

The role of the fund administrator

In the early days of fund administrators the primary role was to carry out the task of the independent calculation of the NAV, independent in the sense that it was not the fund manager who was carrying out the valuation.

Given the diversity and breadth of funds in the market today, the fund administrator's role has somewhat changed. A fund owner appointing an administrator is likely to expect at least the following core functions to be able to be covered by the prospective firm.

Ensuring that the operation of the fund is efficient
NAV Calculation
Publication of the NAV
Maintaining accounts and records
Preparing the audit file

- Liaising with
  (a) the auditor
  (b) the fund manager
  (c) the custodian
  (d) brokers and prime brokers
  (e) limited liability partners
  (f) regulatory authorities
  (g) exchanges (listed funds)
- Performing the role of the registrar
  (a) dealing with investors
  (b) transfer agent – keeping records of purchases and redemptions of shares or units in the fund.
  (c) Managing the annual general meeting including

- – sending out notices
- – preparing agenda and resolutions
- – keeping the minutes of the meeting
- – publishing the report of the meeting etc.
- Calculating
  - (a) Payments and subscription amounts due
  - (b) Arranging/reconciling payments and subscriptions made/ received
  - (c) Fees payable
  - (d) Performance fees (if applicable)
  - (e) Fees chargeable
  - (f) Expenses
- Payment of dividends and distributions
- Maintaining the statutory books and records of the fund
- Money Laundering due diligence
- Ensuring the directors/managers comply with the offering memo- randum or prospectus

In addition, for a hedge fund, the administrator will also be likely to be asked to arrange the setting up of the fund, i.e. registration, legal incorporation, issuing prospectuses, offering memorandum, etc.

We will look at some of these functions in more detail later in this chapter and also in the next chapter.

The key thing about the fund administrator is the relationship with the fund manager.

The administrator must have an excellent understanding of the fund's objectives, the manager's style and the strategies to be used. This will enable value-added services to be developed and provided, adding to the efficiency and overall performance of the fund.

Reconciliation

Amongst many reconciliations associated with a fund's business, the fund administrator performs a key control feature. The task of calcu- lating the NAV requires the asset position of the fund, which in turn needs the confirmation that this asset position agrees with the port- folio the manager believe they have. Without this reconciliation there is likelihood that an incorrect NAV per share will be published.

This task takes place at a stage that is illustrated in Figure 6.1.

Administration workflow

The processes being carried out in the workflow illustrated above start with the transactions in the shares or units of the fund itself. There

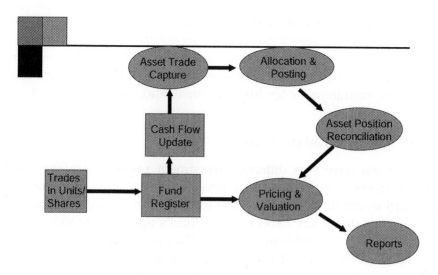

Figure 6.1 Administration Workflow

will be a difference in the volume of activity depending on whether this is a closed- or open-ended fund and whether it is a retail fund, private equity fund or hedge fund, etc. However the accurate recording of the purchases and sales (creation and redemption) of shares and units is vitally important. The task often falls within the remit of the fund registrar or transfer agent.

An important aspect of the fund register maintenance is that it provides vital data relating to cash flow within the fund by showing either a net inflow or outflow of money. We will look at the cash flow issue again later in the book but the important factor here is whether there is a need, as a result of an outflow of cash caused by redemptions of shares or units by investors.

It is not always the case that redemptions of shares or units will create a need for assets in the fund to be converted into cash, e.g. we saw in Chapter 5 how the manager may operate a "box". Also a closed fund will not be subject to the same fluctuation in shares in issue and will therefore not have a cash flow related to purchases and sales of shares.

The cash movements in a fund also include the settlement amounts generated by the purchase and sale of assets by the manager, income like dividends and interest, the result of certain types of corporate actions plus any fees payable, including performance fees to the manager and other accruals for costs and income.

A further key reconciliation concerns the fund's asset positions as per the manager's records and the record of the fund's activities and positions as shown by the custodian or custodians and the prime broker.

The fund register and its cash position are also obviously two vital reconciliations.

Mutual fund administration is different from hedge fund administration in many ways so let us continue looking at the role of the administrator by examining hedge fund administration in greater detail.

Hedge fund administration

Hedge funds have very different investment profiles, strategy, jurisdiction, domicile and legal structures. That said there is a common standard which they must attain in respect of their investors and that is to ensure that every aspect of the fund's operation is managed in a professional and efficient manner. This is vitally important given the nature of the type of investment strategy and the products that might be used by the manager. The investor must be confident that the activity is being monitored and is in line with the fund's offering document.

To the description of the role of the fund administrator given above we can, at its most basic level, say that the hedge fund administrator independently prepares the books and records of the hedge fund. However, hedge fund managers recognise that there is significantly more to the administrator's role than just that function. Like with all funds the administrator is the public face of the manager to the investor and the investment community as a whole. The administrator acts as fiduciary, accountant, agent, consultant and chief operating officer.

It is no longer the case that hedge funds chose their administrator on the basis of personal or previous relationships, as was the case in many instances in certain locations, and today we have a far more professional approach to and requirement for an administrator of a hedge fund. With the increasing investment in hedge funds by institutional investors and sophistication of high net worth private investors, and the consequent depth and breadth of their knowledge, hedge fund managers need to be much more diligent in their research and appointment of the administrator.

What are the main requirements for a hedge fund administrator?

Certainly right at the top is the quality of the management and operational staff. The administrator needs to have qualified staff, preferably with experience gained in the alternative investment industry. It is crucial that they are familiar with industry practice, capital structures, global accounting principles, performance fee and equalisation calculations plus the complexities of the many financial instruments and assets that might be used in the fund.

The administrator's systems need to be able to process and handle long- and short-positions, bonds, equities and currencies, futures, forwards, options, swaps and other derivatives based on those products as well as multiple asset classes including but not restricted to structured products, credit derivatives, property and property derivatives and commodities. Exposure and hedging strategies must be fully understood.

In a typical arrangement the administrator will make a dedicated contact person available to the manager for day-to-day communication about the fund. This person will need to be somebody who is obviously efficient, responsive and easily accessible but they must also under-stand the fund and its activity. Another important issue is the location of the administrator and, if the fund is located somewhere else geographically, whether language is likely to be a problem in any communication.

A major concern for any hedge fund manager in the selection process would be retention levels of staff. Likewise the commitment to training of personnel, services and systems development and investment in the business will all be very crucial considerations. To this we could also add types of funds already serviced.

Whether the administrator has good legal staff and/or access to suitable legal contacts is also very important, especially during the start-up phase. This also extends to the legal expertise and contacts in the international context depending on where the fund is to be registered and/or sold.

Structure

The administrator's internal infrastructure and its situation in the domicile matter. For instance which regulatory authorities supervise its activities, and how? Is it authorised in all of the jurisdictions in which it operates?

How the administrator sets up its internal structure is another issue. The administrator will have various accounts to deal with and would have structured the operational area according to the services it offers and the systems, procedures and processes it manages. There could be individual and distinct departments, for instance accounting, transfer agency, etc. The single points of contact that is offered to the hedge fund managers must be able to resolve and assist with any issues that arise in a timely and effective manner and must be able to handle the number of accounts assigned to them. Further issues of concern to a prospective customer of the administrator might be:

- Disaster recovery/business continuity capabilities – a copy of a tested and audited business continuity and disaster recovery plan may be required.
- Growth – can the administrator handle any growth in the fund's size and activity?
- Is the administrator independent – no possible conflict of interest?
- Will it be able to act in the best interests of the investors in the fund?

Independence is of paramount importance particularly with increasing appetite for more transparency, and in the role of fiduciary agent to the shareholders of the fund, the administrator must be able to demonstrate that its actions and decisions are conducted in the shareholders' best interests.

Crucial to the context of independence is the ability of the administrator to be capable of operating effectively with any prime broker(s), lawyers and auditors, etc.

Global reach and location

A relationship between a hedge fund manager and the administrator is very important one so location of the administrator becomes one related to region. A global administrator, like a global custodian, must be able to accommodate both investors and fund managers in a similar time zone as well as being able to provide a variety of solutions for funds in which the parties are spread across multiple time zones. The principal issue with time zones relates to when there is a problem with the fund operation. Ease of access becomes crucial and problems with communicating or major efforts to liaise with an administrator on the other side of the world tend to divert the manager from their main focus which is of course managing and trading the assets in the fund.

Business considerations

For a prospective customer of a hedge fund administrator it is important to consider whether or not hedge fund administration is the core business and primary focus or merely a product of a far larger organisation. Moving administrator is not something to be contemplated unless absolutely essential and so some kind of demonstration of the long-term commitment to the administration business will almost certainly be needed.

The hedge fund manager will also want to establish how long the service provider has been in the alternative investment business because whilst the administrator may have an excellent track record in administering funds and established a track record supporting long-only mutual funds and is it only just entering the hedge fund sector, then the track record needs to be viewed in a different light.

A hedge fund-specific administrator will be more familiar with the complexities and requirements of the strategies of the managers but the business model of the administrator is another key consideration. It is probable that the administrator must achieve high volumes at low cost if it is to be profitable and must have sufficient business to create the necessary structure and standards. In establishing this critical mass, however, the temptation for many service providers is to take on business for its own sake, which can, but does not have to, invariably result in a disjointed client base that it may struggle to support.

An administrator must be prepared to turn away new business if the capacity to service that business is not available, thus preventing the dilution and deterioration of the service to the existing customers. The administrator should be asking as many questions about the manager and its strategy as the manager would about the fund administrator. Due diligence by the administrator is important so the administrator should be careful to establish whether the client is of the quality, type and class of fund it targets and is one it can properly support.

Technology

No fund administrator and certainly no hedge fund administrator can ignore the issue of technology. Equally a hedge fund will seek some kind of demonstration of the commitment to developing technology-based services. These will include reliable and proven technology and adaptable systems, as well as Web-delivered products and capabilities.

The administrator will either develop in-house capability or will source capability externally. How systems are sourced and developed and the ability to have proprietary systems tailored to the needs of various types of fund serviced is a major management issue and demands significant resource in terms of people and finance.

As a result of their pivotal role in delivering a timely and accurate NAV, hedge fund administrators need to be offering fully automated processes. The minimum level must be to have an integrated portfolio, general ledger and partnership accounting system, which can handle multiple currencies and has direct electronic interfaces with the major prime brokers.

As a result of these electronic data feeds the administrator will receive all necessary information in a timely and efficient manner so that he can calculate the NAV within pre-agreed deadlines. The extent to which manual processes are necessary should be minimised and because they are more prone to error, the administrator must have high degrees of control in place to ensure the number of these errors are at a very low level.

As with all fund administration there must be independent pricing feeds and corporate actions information from a range of sources and where necessary the hedge fund administrator must have the ability to obtain supplementary pricing sources, and to obtain prices for unquoted instruments from independent market-makers and brokers or other appropriate sources.

The accounting processes and systems that are operated by the administrator need to be, first of all, relevant to the customer and meet the required accounting standards and, secondly, must be automated to the degree that information can be disseminated to the manager and investors in the fund promptly.

Fees

A hedge fund manager may need to justify to the fund's share-holders why a particular administrator has been chosen. Cost is an issue but it is not the most important issue, as service standards, depth and suitability are. The fee structure that the administrator proposes must obviously be competitive but although in many cases the fees proposed by administrators are similarly and competitively priced, the product offering between them can vary significantly. This means that the hedge fund manager needs to carefully evaluate the strengths and weaknesses of the various providers as well as the fee structure.

Here the administrator needs to be careful. The fees must be relevant to the service provided and cost of the service provided. Hedge fund managers want to see transparency in the fee structure, in other words no hidden fees. There may be a case for a structure based on percentage of the value of the assets administered plus perhaps a usage fee for specialist or tailored services for the particular fund. These might include preparation of tax data for instance. There must of course be a minimum fee for the service.

The potential client needs to be sure that services are not being charged for that which are actually already provided elsewhere like custody-related services which are provided by the prime broker. Such duplication increases the cost to the fund and the fund sponsors may question the reasons for appointing the administrator.

Fund launches

The administrator's experience with a variety of hedge fund structures and strategies can place it in a very strong position to assist with the launch of the fund. Indeed it can be an invaluable resource in the run-up to a fund's launch.

For instance, in-house lawyers and accountants can assist in reviewing the offering and other constitutional documents, examining them for consistency and making sure they are operational accurate in matters such as performance fee calculation and equalisation methodology.

The administrators can also draw upon their experience to help a sponsor to overcome particular quirks of launching funds in certain jurisdictions.

Other roles of the administrator can have during the preparation of documentation will be to

- Liaise with external auditors
- Liaise with prime brokers
- Liaise with independent legal counsel.

Once the initial offering period begins, the administrator's transfer agency team will liaise with the hedge fund investors. They will send offering documents to all potential investors and ensure that they comply with the regulations. The administrator will receive completed applications and subscription moneys. They will ensure that the documentation is complete and correct and that all necessary 'know your customer' information (including information that is needed to make sure possible money laundering is not taking place) and verifications are supplied and checked.

The administrator will then issue shares or units based on the initial offering price, or on the NAV of the fund if subscriptions are received after the initial offering period.

The method used by the administrator to communicate with the investors is therefore crucial, particularly where a geographically diverse investor base exists.

The investor will expect to receive timely information on, amongst other things:

- The latest fund information
- Statements on current holdings
- Transaction history statements
- The status of pending subscriptions and redemption orders.

We can see here that an administrator's ability to provide an investor with Web-based, online access is a distinct advantage.

The ability to provide an easy and continuous access facility removes the need for administratively costly and inconvenient communications methods, like paper statements, with investors locally and globally.

Accounting

The NAV calculation begins with downloading the trade activity of the manager which will come from either a custodian or a prime broker. Ideally the administrator should have an automated electronic feed established and this feed will in turn download each day's trades from the broker to the administrator.

Once received it is input into the systems of the administrator to produce a daily portfolio statement. The administrator will then receive data about corporate actions like dividend announcements, prices, etc supplied by various vendors into its database. The portfolio is then updated to include accrued dividends, interest, fees, charges, etc. Automatic reconciliation should then match the portfolio to the trades fed from the manager, or to portfolios produced by the back office of a bank or broker.

Today the ability to establish the portfolio changes, receive the data, and produce the NAV and other accounting information quickly is more and more important as the need for daily and even intra-day NAVs increases.

Many hedge funds that once had monthly NAVs now need daily ones calculated and even if they are still produced monthly the turn around needs to be far more rapid.

Other reporting includes a full set of financial statements, including a statement of assets and liabilities, a statement of transactions, a statement of changes in net assets and a summary portfolio.

Some information produced will be in the form of portfolio analysis and other statistics of interest to the manager. As a result the administrator may become involved in reporting related to areas such as comparisons to benchmarks.

Naturally tax accounting services are very much required.

Compliance services

The fund employs the manager and administrator and so the fund therefore delegates its compliance including mandate checks and anti-money laundering checks to the administrator. The administrator is therefore the entity responsible for verifying the details of the investors and as the administrator must act in the best interests of the investor he must ensure that the fund's activities remain firmly within the confines detailed in its prospectus and constitutive documents. He must also ensure that all investors are treated equally where required, and that all necessary filings and fees are submitted in a timely manner to the various regulatory authorities and stock exchanges.

Summary

With hedge fund administration and indeed mutual fund administration the key thing is the quality and depth of the experience of the people and capability of the systems.

Experienced personnel, staff with real product knowledge and understanding of the investment and fund process and sophisticated systems are central to successful fund administration.

7

Portfolio administration

The activity of the fund manager in the markets and the buying and selling activity of the investor mean that the positions within the portfolio are subject to change, sometimes quite frequent change. The portfolio record must be constantly updated to reflect these changes and the proper accounting entries and records maintained.

There are several key areas of portfolio administration that need to be considered and these include:

- Records of the assets held within the portfolio
- Records of changes to the assets held
- Income and benefits accruing from the assets
- Records of the expenses, fees and costs payable out of the fund
- Valuations of the total assets of the fund (sometimes referred to as the property)
- Records of the purchase and sales of units or shares in the fund by investors
- Records of any distribution of income or dividend to investors
- Records of any performance-related fees due to the manager
- The tax situation pertaining to the fund.

The importance of the proper maintenance of the records of the fund is fairly obvious. For instance, the accurate calculation of the value of the fund, the NAV, and the publication of the fund price, the NAV per share, are essential and are covered by various regulatory requirements.

Equally the proper record of the fund register of investors and their holding is vital for both the calculation of the NAV and the distribution of any income.

Assets of the fund

The fund manager invests the inflow of cash received from investors into assets that are held in the portfolio. The basis for the investment is determined by the asset allocation and stock selection process applicable to the fund. For example, if the fund asset allocation profile is as shown in the following table then the inflow of funds is distributed across the assets classes. The stock selector then selects the actual asset that will be purchased.

Asset class	Benchmark allocation (%)	Tactical allocation (%)
Equity	50	30–70
Debt	25	15–35
Other	20	0–40
Cash	5	2–10

Every time the manager purchases or sells assets the portfolio must be updated to reflect the new position in terms of:

- Assets held
- Cash held.

Where investors sell more units or shares than there are buyers on the other side, the manager may be selling or liquidating assets in order to generate cash flow to pay the investors the amounts they are due. For example:

The current allocation of assets (weighting) in the portfolio is as follows.

Asset class	Allocation (%)
Equity	60
Debt	20
Other	15
Cash	5

The manager is notified of a net incoming cash flow of £100,000. Given the current weighting the £100,000 will be invested as:

- £60,000 in equities
- £20,000 in debt

- £15,000 in others
- £5000 held in cash.

If the net cash flow was outflow the manager would look to generate the funds through a reduction in each asset class according to the weighting. The manager may also look to other means of generating the cash flow needed to meet outflows of investment to avoid disruption to the portfolio. For instance the fund may have the ability to borrow but the terms of that authority to borrow, the borrowing powers, may or may not preclude its use for redemption of shares or units.

The following figure, which we originally saw in the previous chapter, shows the generic process flows associated with a fund:

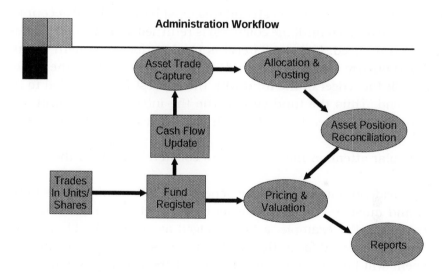

We can see that the activity of the investors leads to a cash flow update that the manger acts on. As the manager buys or sells assets the ledgers need to be updated with the resultant trades and associated payments. These will include:

- Subscriptions
- Redemptions
- Asset purchases
- Asset sales
- Commission, costs and fees
- Taxes (where applicable)
- Dividend, interest and other income
- Distribution of income to investors.

In addition there are other entries that will be necessary for some types of products, e.g. derivatives where a margin call is made.

Margin and collateral

Some derivatives like futures contracts have a margin call that is payable by the fund to their broker as part of the risk management process in the market. Where futures are used we must establish a margin account in the fund records to record the value of the margin deposited with the broker. As collateral is used, either cash or assets, it is important that the records accurately reflect the amount of collateral the fund is being required to deposit and that this collateral remains an asset of the fund. Where cash is used as collateral there will be interest paid by the broker on that cash and this must be agreed and accounted for through accrual until the collateral is returned and the total interest has been received. If the collateral is in place for any length of time and particularly over a month end, the probability is that the broker will credit the ledger of the fund with the interest for the period to the month end. Thus the fund can accrue the interest until month end and then post the receipt of the cash flow associated with the interest payment.

Particular attention must be paid to collateral that is in the form of assets.

Any dividend, interest or other benefit or entitlement belongs to the fund and must be accounted for as if the asset were not being used as collateral. For example, a bond lodged as collateral will still have the interest accrued for in the fund's accounts. Likewise any dividend payment will be received either directly if the security is still in the fund's name or by payment from the broker if the security has been transferred into the broker's name. As there can be tax issues related to income that is not directly received it is prudent to either pledge the collateral, in which case the security is not transferred, or when a dividend is due alternative collateral is used so that the security is reinstated in the fund's name to the custodian.

Asset trades

Asset trades in the portfolio occur for two reasons. First, the investor activity described above and secondly as a result of the manager's strategic decisions on the makeup of the actual assets being held.

Remember that the manager is seeking to deliver a return in the fund and that return is usually benchmarked. In most cases other than tracker funds, the manager is looking to outperform the benchmark either through tactical asset allocation and/or stock selection.

As a result the manager is using research information either from in-house sources or external parties like brokers, or indeed both and is switching from one asset to another or adding to or reducing the holding in an asset or asset class as appropriate (see table below).

Asset class – Equity			
Market	Sector	Holding	Action
UK	Energy	BP	Buy 50,000
US	Energy	Exxon	Sell 10,000

The stock selectors based on their research analysis decide to increase the holding of BP and reduce the holding of Exxon. This results in trades that must be captured and recorded in the portfolio records so that the new portfolio position is correctly shown.

		Asset class – Equity			
Market	Sector	Holding	Previous	New	Change
UK	Energy	BP	500,000	550,000	+50,000
		Shell	1,500,000	1,500,000	
Europe					
US		Exxon	300,000	290,000	–10,000
Asia-Pacific					
	Sector total		2,300,000	2,340,000	

Income and entitlements

The assets held in the portfolio will or may generate certain income or other entitlements that again must be recognised and properly accounted for in the portfolio records. The most common incidences of these entitlements relate to dividend and interest on equity and bonds respectively. However other types of corporate action may result in a need to update the portfolio record, for instance a bonus issue on an equity share or an early redemption on a bond.

Remember that whilst the custodian may be actually dealing with the corporate action the position in the manager's record must be updated and reconciled.

Using the same table as before if a corporate action such as a 2 for 1 capitalisation or bonus issue occurred on the holding in BP the position would again change:

Asset class – Equity					
Market	Sector	Holding	Previous	New	Change
UK	Energy	BP	550,000	1,100,000	+550,000
		Shell	1,500,000	1,500,000	
Europe					
US		Exxon	290,000	290,000	
Asia-Pacific					
	Sector total		2,300,000	2,890,000	

The implication of not updating the fund record is illustrated by incorporating the price and value as shown below.

Asset class – Equity							
Market	Sector	Holding	Previous	New	Change	Price	Value
UK	Energy	BP	550,000	550,000		£2.25	£1,237,500
		Shell	1,500,000	1,500,000		£6.00	£9,000,000
						Total	£10,235,000
Europe							0
						Total	0
US		Exxon	300,000	290,000		$20	$5,800,000
						Total	$5,800,000
Asia-Pacific							
	Sector Total		2,300,000	2,340,000			

				Correct Position			
				Asset class – Equity			
Market	Sector	Holding	Previous	New	Change	Price	Value
UK	Energy	BP	550,000	1,100,000	+550,000	£2.25	£2,475,000
		Shell	1,500,000	1,500,000		£6.00	£9,000,000
						Total	£11,475,000
Europe							0
						Total	0
US		Exxon	290,000	290,000		$20	$5,800,000
						Total	$5,800,000
Asia-Pacific							0
						Total	0
	Sector Total		2,300,000	2,890,000			

What we can very easily see is that the valuation is incorrect in the first table and if this was used in the NAV calculation the value of the fund is understated by £1,237,500, i.e. half the real value of the holding.

As the custodian's record will be changed the reconciliation process should, provided it is timely, prevent the erroneous valuation and publication of the fund price.

The reconciliation that we are talking about is shown in the following figure:

Reconciliation

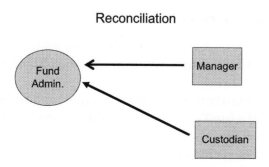

If the fund is a hedge fund or is a fund using a prime broker's services then the following figure would apply:

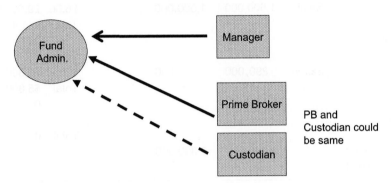

Reconciliation

Fund administrator is reconciling to the manager, prime broker and possibly the custodian

The major issue here is that the flow of data on the activity of the manager and the updating of the positions held at the custodian is vitally important as far as the administrator is concerned. The position as far as the fund is concerned is created when the manager does a trade in the market. The custodian will update the position according to the settlement process at the central securities depository or the clearing house (unless contractual date settlement accounting is being applied). As a result the custodian may be showing a different position to that of the manager. The transaction may be:

- Unmatched

or

- Unsettled

Unmatched transactions

These can be an issue. A transaction that is unmatched in the market could result in either a cancellation or an amendment to the original transaction.

This has an implication for the NAV calculation and therefore of the published price of a fund's share. Depending on whether this is a significant size transaction it may or may not have a significant impact on the fund value. A cancellation may result in another trade at a different price and an amended price will create a different value, but it is possible that the ultimate difference may be very small.

Most unmatched trades will be resolved quickly, often in just a few minutes and the administrator may not even be aware that there was an unmatched trade.

However an unmatched trade could become a major problem if the manager is not aware of the problem and is therefore not addressing the issue or is aware but is simply not dealing with it.

If the product concerned is say a derivative then the implications become far greater and the administrator needs to escalate the issue so that resolution is achieved.

A significant change could result in a •pricing error that may need reporting.

Unsettled transactions

These may also prove to be an issue but are often merely a delay in achieving settlement rather than resulting in a change to the transaction itself.

However the settlement failure could result in a •buy in in the market and therefore result in a price change. Again this is only likely to be a problem if the price is significantly altered.

Claims

A bigger issue for the fund is to ensure that any cost that is created by a late or altered settlement is claimed from the originator. The custodian will almost certainly be providing this service but it is important that the administrator is monitoring that this is being dealt with and any costs reclaimed is credited to the fund.

8

NAV, pricing and valuations

Calculating the NAV of a fund is a key task of the administrator.

De"nition of Net Asset Value

The net asset value (NAV) of a fund can be described in simplistic form as the assets minus the fund's liabilities.

The NAV equals the fund's total value such that if a fund had assets with a total value of £75 million and the total liabilities (fees, costs and charges) were say £15 million then the net value of the fund would be £60 million. Once the NAV has been determined the NAV per share can be calculated by dividing the value by the number of shares or units issued by the fund. Thus if the fund had 1,500,000 shares/units issued to investors the NAV per share would equal £50.

Why is the NAV important? This number is important to investors for the simple reason that it is from the NAV that the price per unit of a fund is calculated. By dividing the NAV of a fund by the number of outstanding shares/units the price per share/unit is established. If the NAV is incorrect the NAV per share is incorrect and investors buying or selling shares/units could end up paying or receiving less or more than they should have.

The NAV of most funds constantly changes as the asset values change and the managers increase or decrease, or simply change the allocation of the assets in the fund. This change is more often than not reflected in a daily calculation of the assets/liabilities. This is certainly the case with most mutual funds and unit trusts in the retail market and is also the case for some hedge funds especially those included in funds of hedge funds. The NAVs of some funds are calculated less frequently either because they are hedge funds with low numbers of investors and little buying/selling activity in the shares of the fund or because they hold assets that cannot be realistically valued on a day-to-day basis. Property for instance is an example of an asset class that cannot be valued on a day-to-day basis.

As the NAV is constantly changing it must be published to investors and so the administrator must advise the manager on the NAV and the NAV per share. The manager is responsible for publishing the NAV and should check the calculation total for •reasonableness . Funds have set times when the NAV calculation and publication of share/unit prices takes place but different funds can have various times on when they do this. Often it is the end of each trading day when the recalculation of NAV and fund share/unit takes place.

The NAV is a snap shot value of the fund and is not an indication of performance. This is because many funds are constantly paying out distributions of income and sometimes capital growth. Open-ended funds also fluctuate in terms of the amount under management.

To illustrate why the NAV does not represent the growth or decline in value from a performance point of view we can look at the following illustration.

If a fund's NAV grows from £5 to £10 it would appear that a 100 per cent growth has been achieved. However if during this period a distribution of income has occurred of say £2.50 the fund's real performance is 150 per cent.

So the NAV of a fund is the fund's total assets minus its total liabilities and the NAV will most likely change each day.

Retail funds generally must calculate their NAV at least once every business day. A closed fund, where the manager is not issuing or canceling shares/units, may calculate its value less frequently. An investment trust company in the UK is not valued by calculation of an NAV but the shares, listed on an exchange, trade at the price in the market.

An open-ended investment company calculates the NAV of a single share (or the •per share NAV) by dividing its NAV by the number of shares that are outstanding. Because the NAV per share is based on NAV which changes daily and on the number of shares held by investors, which also changes daily, per share NAV also will change daily. Most mutual funds publish their per share NAVs in the daily newspapers or possibly on their website. The unit funds and traditional

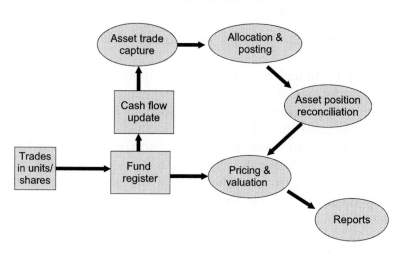

Figure 8.1

unit trust is based on a bid and offer price based around the NAV of the trust.

The NAV process takes place as part of the overall fund administration workflow as shown in Figure 8.1.

Pricing of funds

The price that investors receive on redemptions is the NAV per share at the time of redemption minus any fees that the fund deducts at that time (such as loads, dilution levy, etc). Likewise the price of the fund's shares/units to the buyer is the NAV per share at the time of purchase plus any fees, charges, etc.

Intuition tells us that a mutual fund's NAV, the net value of all assets within the fund less the liabilities and accruals divided by the number of shares issued, should be identical to its market price. But often the market price of a closed-end fund, a fund with a fixed number of issued shares which cannot be altered, will trade either above or below its NAV. When this situation occurs and the fund is trading above its NAV it is trading at a premium and if it is below the NAV it is trading at a discount.

Why does it trade at a different price?

Here are some possible reasons why these funds would trade at a premium or a discount:

- The fundamentals of supply and demand will adjust the trading price.
- If the fund is in high demand and low supply, then the market price will typically exceed the NAV.
- If there is low demand and much supply, then the market price will usually be lower than the NAV.
- The management team responsible for the fund itself because if the manager is highly regarded, a premium may be paid by investors wishing to hold the fund (if the management is not as highly regarded, there is a possibility that the fund may trade at a discount).
- Expectation – similar to a stock, the expectation that all fund will perform well may affect whether the market price is above or below the NAV.

Hedge fund pricing

Hedge fund managers actively manage investment portfolios with a goal of absolute returns regardless of overall market or index movements. They do however use trading strategies with more freedom than a retail mutual fund or unit trust. They are not usually registered with a regulator and so do not have to comply with the types of pricing rules described above.

Hedge fund values are obviously related to the type of strategy and products used. The administrator should remember that higher returns are certainly not guaranteed and it would be unwise to assume a pricing problem if the value of the fund has fallen. Most hedge funds invest in the same securities available to mutual funds and unit trust managers but may adopt the use of derivatives and other products to achieve gearing or leverage. Depending on the manager's strategy the calculation of the NAV of a hedge fund may therefore be virtually identical to that for a mutual fund and present very little in the way of problems for the administrator.

One area that will be different is the inclusion of performance fees and the need to accrue for the fee in the NAV calculations. The basis for the performance fee will have been included in the offering documents and will include detail of what hurdles there may be and also the high watermark principle where the manager must exceed the previous high in the fund's value to earn more performance-related compensation.

Pricing assets

The major issue for the administrator is the liquidity of the instrument and availability of a robust price source.

Most listed securities cause little problem as the exchange becomes the price source. Many single price funds use a •mid price to value the securities assets in the portfolio and this is absolutely fine provided that some form of dilution levy or similar is applied to make sure that there is no •cost to buyer or seller. Securities in dual-priced unit trusts can be priced on a bid-and-offer basis to create the right creation and cancellation price for the units, otherwise some form of dilution miti-gation will be needed. On-exchange derivatives offer little in the way of problem as again the exchange serves as the price source, however the impact of the derivatives' instruments must be included in the correct asset classes for both accounting and portfolio valuation purposes.

Off-exchange of over-the-counter (OTC) transactions present more of an issue. Some are high liquid products that also trade on exchange so a price source is available. Others are more bespoke, less liquid and may have no obvious source of price other than the counterparty of a specifically developed pricing model. As the latter, because of cost and/or complexity, is only likely to be found in the largest of banks it is vitally important that the fund owners/sponsors, manager(s) and the administrator agree on a •pricing policy that will be used for those instruments that have no, limited or doubtful sources of price.

The prospectus or offering documents will outline the pricing policy, including frequency of the NAV calculations, when and where the price of the shares/units will be published, etc.

Pricing controls

The pricing policy (Figure 8.2) is important but so too are the pricing controls.

The list below gives some of the pricing controls one might expect to be implemented by the administrator to meet trustee, depositary or regulatory requirements.

Example of pricing controls

- Reliability of source of price and rates should be continuously reviewed for appropriateness and accuracy
- Any third-party systems used must be robust and produce consis-tent and accurate results
- Valuation output should be agreed to the managers records at each valuation point

Illustration of a Pricing Policy

The fund has a pricing policy, the following are the main features.

(1) The fund will use market prices, either official closing or indicative prices at a set time where markets are still open, whenever available.

(2) The mid price will be used when bids and offers are quoted.

(3) For unlisted securities the fund will use a formula that applies reasonableness checks on prices available that takes into account liquidity, comparable securities etc.

(4) Foreign exchange and interest rates will be taken from the 3rd party vendor information system (e.g. Bloomberg, Reuters).

(5) OTC derivatives prices will be taken from the 3rd party vendor information system (e.g. Bloomberg, Reuters), or the in-house pricing models.

(6) Where there is neither a vendor system nor in-house model for a product the price source and price used will be determined by the Pricing Committee (the pricing committee is formed of directors of the company, the fund manager and the fund administrator).

(7) Where appropriate, and if the Pricing Committee determines, there will be a panel of 3rd party brokers who will be asked for a valuation. The highest and lowest will be discarded and the remainder averaged to determine the price to be used.

(8) The Pricing Committee may in exceptional circumstances, such as bespoke, structured products use a price based solely on the assessment of the fund managers and/or counterparty to the transaction.

(9) The robustness and reliability of the source of prices, valuation processes and systems and the effectiveness of the pricing controls and procedures will be continuously monitored by the fund administrator and by the directors of the fund and amended appropriately in relation to the activity and products within the fund.

Source: The Derivatives and Securities Consultancy Ltd

Figure 8.2

- Managers/ACD records should be agreed to the depositary/trustee records monthly
- Checks should include debtors and prospect of recovery
- Deals completed prior to the valuation date should be included
- Deals completed up to 1 hour before the valuation point should be included
- Documented and monitored procedures to ensure compliance with these requirements must be in place.
- Where a price source/method other than the normal documented price source is used a record of the reason, basis and source for the price should be maintained
- The administrator should ensure as part of the pricing process that any borrowing powers of the fund have not been exceeded
- There must be adequate checks to ensure that all accruals for income (dividend, interest, etc) and fees (charges, costs, performance fees, etc) have been made in the calculation process
- Reviewing the tax position of the fund periodically
- Reviewing the basis and justification for the frequency of dealing, dealing expenses and commissions and concentration of counterparty

- A system of exceptions should be introduced either on a fixed percentage or absolute limit to highlight exceptional movement in value of individual assets and/or total portfolio valuation movement
- Results of investigation into the exceptions should be documented and be looked at in terms of
  - Overall value of fund
  - Movement in individual assets
  - Changes in currency rates
  - Accruals of income and/or expenses
  - Tax
- Asset prices that are unaltered for more than a period of say 4 days should be investigated
- The cash position in the fund should be reconciled
- Procedures and checks to reconcile shares/units in issue are accurate in the calculation
- Manager should check the valuations as frequently as is appropriate
- Errors in valuation must be reported to the manager, trustee and depositary and if a published price is affected then where applicable compensation may have to be paid to investors (for some funds this is typically a pricing error of 0.5 per cent of the price of the unit or share)

In general terms the administrator MUST:

- Have adequate pricing capability for the assets held in the portfolios
- Document the pricing policy adopted
- Document any pricing issue
- Liaise with the manager and trustee/depositary immediately an error/issue is discovered
- Be prepared to recalculate the value if the manager is doubtful about its accuracy

Equalisation

What is equalisation?

There are two issues surrounding this subject. First, we can consider the investor buying units in a unit trust and, secondly, we can look at the issue surrounding investors buying into a hedge fund.

If we look at a unit trust invested in bonds we can have a situation as shown in Figure 8.3.

What has happened here is that the investors buying into the fund during the income period are paying both capital to invest in the units and also paying for the interest accrued since the last income distribution date on the bonds in the portfolio. Equalisation shows the amount of the

Example:
There are 120,000 units at a subscription of 50p each which are in the portfolio that has a fixed income security that has a 12% coupon.
No capital appreciation is assumed and there are two new investors joining the fund on the last day of month 2 and 4, each subscribing 10,000 units

End of Month	Group 1 Units	Group 2 Units	Income G1	Income G2	Price of Units	Equalisation	Capital
0	100,000				0.500		50,000
1	100,000		500		0.505		
2		10,000			0.510	100	5,000
2	100,000	10,000	500		0.510		
3	100,000	10,000	500	50	0.515		
4		10,000			0.520		
4	100,000	20,000	500	50	0.520	200	5,000
5	100,000	20,000	500	100	0.525		
6	100,000	20,000	500	100	0.530		
			3,000	300	0.530	300	60,000

Distribution will be 120,000 units at 3p per unit. The value is £3600 made up of the £3000 income from G1 units, £300 from G2 units and £ 300 being the amount of equalisation out of the subscription amount (the price included accrued interest) of the two new investors.

After the distribution the price per unit returns to 50p and all 120,000 units are now G1 units going into the next income period.

The actual distribution was therefore made up of £3000 to G1 units that is all income and £600 to G2 units which is half income and half equalisation.

Source: Securities and Investment Institute

Figure 8.3

price of the units that was represented by accrued interest and which was the capital. This can have implications for the investors' tax situation.

With hedge funds the main features of equalisation in relation to performance fees are to achieve a single NAV by means of adjusting the share balance at the end of the period of the calculation of the performance fee. An alternative is to have a Series of Shares which then means that every time a new investment is made a new series of shares is created and a separate NAV for each series is maintained. The new shares are consolidated into the ordinary shares at the end of the period if a performance fee has been triggered.

The simplest way of all for the administrator is for the performance fee to be calculated at fund level but this can lead to inequalities for different investors and can lead to the manager •working for nothing to raise an investors' share value to the previous high watermark.

To illustrate this we can look at the following situation as shown in Figure 8.4.

The above illustration is based on one contained in a presentation by Dermot Butler at Custom House, a Dublin-based fund

Equalisation: "The free ride"

1	Investor A buys one share at £100
2	End of Qtr1 GNAV p s = £110
3	Published NAV = £108
4	High watermark = £110
5	End of month NAV = £100
6	Investor B buys one share at £100
7	High watermark still £110
8	Investor B has a £2 "free ride" to £110

Figure 8.4a

Equalisation: "Subsidising"

1	Investor A buys one share at £100
2	GNAV p s = £110
3	Published NAV = £108
4	Investor B buys one share at £108
5	Qtr End GNAV = £120
6	Gross profit = £32
7	Incentive fee = 20% of £32 = £3.20 per share
8	Investor A pays 16.4% on £20 profit, investor B pays 26.66% on £12 profit

Figure 8.4b

administrator. The full document can be accessed at their website (see Appendices).

Summary

Pricing and valuations present many challenges for the administrator. Knowledge of the products being used and how they derive their values is obviously important. Knowing the best sources of reliable prices, having adequate pricing policy and controls is also vital and above all understanding what the manager is doing and being able to know whether a increase or decrease in value is likely help the administrator to monitor the accuracy of the calculations.

Discipline, accuracy and knowledge – these are the key things.

NAV is important and errors will damage the administrator as well as the fund's reputation. Compensation for significant errors will be needed and if this is caused by the administrator not doing the task properly the fund is likely to seek compensation themselves and will certainly look to replace the administrator!

Glossary

30/360	Also 360/360, 30(E)/360 or accrual basis. A day/year count convention assuming 30 days in each calendar month and a 'year' of 360 days; adjusted in America for certain periods ending on 31st day of the month (and then sometimes known as 30(A)/360).
AAA	The highest credit rating for a company or asset – the risk of default is negligible.
Absolute interest	The legal ownership and beneficial ownership of an asset by the same person.
Accreting swap	A swap where the notional principal increases during the life of the swap.
Accumulation units or shares	Shares or units in a fund where the distributed income is reinvested.
Accrual basis	See 30/360.
Accrued interest	Interest due on a bond or other fixed income security that must be paid by the buyer of a security to its seller. The amount of accrued interest is the coupon times the days elapsed since the last coupon payment date.
ACT/360	A day/year count convention taking the number of calendar days in a period and a 'year' of 360 days.

ACT/365	Also ACT/365 Fixed or ACT/365-F. A day/year count convention taking the number of calendar days in a period and a 'year' of 365 days. Under the ISDA definitions used for interest rate swap documentation, ACT/365 means the same as ACT/ACT.
ACT/365 Fixed	See ACT/365.
ACT/365-F	See ACT/365.
ACT/ACT	For an interest rate swap, a day/year count convention dividing the number of calendar days in the interest period that fall in a leap year by 366 and dividing the remainder by 365.
Actual settlement date	Date the transaction effectively settles in the clearing house (exchange of securities eventually against cash).
Affirmation	Affirmation refers to the counterparty's agreement with the terms of the trade as communicated.
Agency bond	A bond issued by, for example, a quasi-governmental US agency, such as one of the government national mortgage corporations.
Agent bank	A commercial bank that provides services as per their client's instructions.
Agent	One who executes orders for or otherwise acts on behalf of another (the principal) and is subject to its control and authority. The agent takes no financial risk and may receive a fee or commission.
All or none (AON)	Instruction to buy or sell the entire order in a single transaction, i.e. not to execute a partial transaction. AON restricts the size but not necessarily the time of the transaction.
Allocation (give up)	The process of moving the trade from the executing broker to the clearing broker in exchange-traded derivatives.
Allotment	The amount of new issues (i.e. number of bonds, shares) given to a syndicate member by the lead manager. Also the amount of an issue allotted to a subscribing investor.

Alpha A measurement of the value that an investment manager produces by comparing the manager's performance to that of a risk-free investment such as a Treasury Bill. An alpha of 1.0 for a fund during a month would show that the return produced was one percentage point higher than that of the benchmark treasury.

Alpha can also be used to measure the residual risk relative to the market that the fund participates in.

Alternative investment market (AIM) Second tier of market run by the London Stock Exchange where smaller, growing companies are listed without meeting the criteria needed for a listing on the main market.

American depository receipt (ADR) A depository receipt issued by an American bank to promote trading in a foreign stock or share. The bank holds the underlying securities and an American depository is issued against them. The receipt entitles the holder to all dividends and capital gains in USD. ADRs allow investors to purchase foreign stock without having to involve themselves in foreign settlements and currency conversion.

American style option The holder of the long position can choose to exercise the position into the underlying instrument until the expiry day.

Amortisation Accounting procedure that gradually reduces the cost value of a limited life asset or intangible asset through periodic charges to income. The purpose of amortisation is to reflect the resale or redemption value. Amortisation also refers to the reduction of debt by regular payments of interest and principal to pay off a loan by maturity.

Amortising swap A swap where the notional principal decreases during the life of the swap.

Announcement In a new bond issue, the day on which a release is sent to prospective syndicate members describing the offering and inviting underwriters and selling group members to join the syndicate.

Annual (management) fee	A fee charged for the managers' time and costs in managing the investments of the fund, also known as a management fee.
Annual general meeting (AGM)	Meeting of shareholders which a company, including investment funds and unit trusts, must call every year. Main purposes are to receive the accounts, vote on dividends and appoint directors, etc.
Annual rate of return	In fund management, the compounded gain or loss in a fund's net asset value during a calendar year.
Annuity	For the recipient, an arrangement whereby the individual receives a pre-specified payment annually for a pre-specified number of years, for instance from an insurance company in exchange for a lump sum investment.
Arbitrage investment strategy	Taking opposite positions in similar securities or securities and derivatives or in the same instruments traded on different markets to take advantage of pricing anomalies.
Arbitrageur	A trader who takes advantage of profitable opportunities arising from price anomalies.
As agent	One who acts as an intermediary or broker in a transaction and who assumes no financial risk. For this service, the firm receives a stated commission or fee.
Asian option	See average rate option.
Ask price	Price at which a market maker will sell the stock. Also known as the offer price.
Asset allocation	The allocation of the portfolio to various asset classes. Also the use of derivatives by a fund manager to immediately gain or reduce exposure to different markets.
Asset-backed securities	Debt obligations that pay principal and interest; principal only or interest only; deferred interest and negative interest using a combination of factors and rate multipliers. The issues are serviced by multiple vendors that supply the necessary data to make the corresponding payments.

Asset swap	An interest rate swap or currency swap used to change the interest rate exposure and/or the currency exposure of an investment. Also used to describe the package of the swap plus the investment itself.
Assets	Everything of value that is owned or is due: fixed assets (cash, buildings, machinery etc.) and intangible assets (patents, good will etc.).
Assignment	The process by which the holder of a short option position is matched against a holder of a similar long option position who has exercised his right.
Association of British Insurers (ABI)	A trade body of insurance companies through which they can air their views collectively on matters of common concern.
Associate Corporate Director	An authorised director of an open-ended investment company in the UK.
At-the-money	An option whose exercise price is equal, or very close, to the current market price of the underlying share. This option has no intrinsic value.
At best order	Type of order input into SETS which is completed against displayed orders at the best prices(s) available.
ATM	See at-the-money.
Auction	Method by which the Bank of England issues gilts. Successful applicants pay the price that they have offered.
Authentication agent	A bank putting a signature on each physical bond to certify its genuineness prior to the distribution of the definitive bonds on the market.
Authorisation	Status required by the Financial Services and Markets Act 2000 for any firm that wants to conduct investment business.
Authorised Corporate Director (ACD)	Organisation which undertakes the role of managing the funds in an OEIC.
Authorised Unit Trust	Unit trust which meets the requirements of the Financial Services Authority to allow it to be freely marketable.

Average rate option	An option where the settlement is based on the difference between the strike and the average price of the underlying over a predetermined period. Also known as Asian options.
Average strike option	An option that pays the difference between the average rate of the underlying over the life of the option and the rate at expiry.
Back-to-back transaction	See turnaround.
Ballot	A random selection of applicants for a new issue of shares.
Bank – commercial	Organisation that takes deposits and makes loans.
Bank – merchant	Organisation that specialises in advising on takeovers and corporate finance activities.
Bank of England	The UK's central bank which undertakes policy decided by the Treasury and determines interest rates.
Bank for International Settlements	Set up in the 1920s to administer debt repayments among European countries, it now has an important role as the vocal point in organising discussion on International finance.
Bankers' acceptance	Short-term negotiable discount note, drawn on and accepted by banks which are obliged to pay the face value amount at maturity.
Bankruptcy	An individual is deemed bankrupt when he or she is unable to pay their debts. Bankrupt companies go into liquidation or receivership.
Bare trust	A trust where the trustee holds the trust property for a single beneficiary.
Bargain	Another word for a transaction or deal. It does not imply that a particularly favourable price was obtained.
Barrier option	Also trigger option, exploding option or extinguishing option. An option that is either cancelled or activated if the underlying price reaches a predetermined barrier or trigger level. See knock-out option and knock-in option.
Base currency	Currency chosen for reporting purposes.

Base rate	The rate of interest set by the banks as a basis for the rate on loans and deposits.
Basis (gross)	The difference between the relevant cash instrument price and the futures price. Often used in the context of hedging the cash instrument.
Basis (value or net)	The difference between the gross basis and the carry.
Basis Point (BP)	A change in the interest rate of one hundredth of one per cent (0.01%). One basis point is written as 0.01 when 1.0 represents 1%.
Basis risk	The risk that the price or rate of one instrument or position might not move exactly in line with the price or rate of another instrument or position which is being used to hedge it.
Basis swap	An interest rate swap where the interest payment that are exchanged between each party are different types of floating rates.
Bear	Investor who believes prices will fall.
Bear market	A market in which prices are falling, and sellers are more predominant than buyers. Usually refers to equity markets.
Bear raid	The selling of shares, generally in large volumes, to influence the price in order to acquire shares more cheaply.
Bear squeeze	Where a bear investor having gone 'short' and sold more shares than he has in anticipation of either a share or the market as a whole falling is squeezed by the rising price during the speculative period.
Bearer document	Documents which state on them that the person in physical possession (the bearer) is the owner, examples being currency or bearer bonds.
Bearer securities	Unregistered securities where the holder of the certificate is deemed the owner. Income is usually paid on presentation of the coupon.
Benchmark	An index, basket or other measure against which the performance of the fund is assessed
Benchmark bond	The most recently issued and most liquid government bond.

Beneficial owner	The person entitled to all benefits of ownership even though a broker or bank holds the security.
Bermudan option	An option where the holder can choose to exercise on any of a series of predetermined dates between the purchase of the option and the expiry. See American style option, and European style option.
Best-efforts basis	Term describing an instruction received by a broker or custodian recognising that due to factors beyond their control a specific outcome cannot be guaranteed.
Best execution	The requirement for a broker to obtain the best market price when buying or selling a marketable investment on behalf of the client.
Beta coefficient	A measure of the volatility or movement of a share in comparison to the market as a whole.
Bid	(a) The price or yield at which a purchaser is willing to buy a given security. (b) To quote a price or yield at which a purchaser is able to buy a given security. (c) The investor's selling price of units in a unit-linked policy.
Bilateral netting	A netting system in which all trades executed on the same date in the same security between the same counterparties are grouped and netted to one final delivery versus payment.
Bill of exchange	A money market instrument, a written promise to pay a specified sum of money (usually post-dated) that is similar to a cheque.
BIS	Bank for International Settlements.
Block trade	A purchase or sale of a large number of shares or dollar value of bonds normally much more than what constitutes a round lot in the market in question.
Blue chips	Denotes the companies that in theory at least provide the safest equity investment potential. Companies listed on the FT-SE 100 are considered Blue Chip.
Board lot	Standard unit of shares commonly traded in the market. Shares that are issued in fractions or multiples of a board lot are referred to as odd lots and jumbo lots respectively and may not be readily negotiable.

Bond
A certificate of debt, generally long term, under the terms of which an issuer contracts, inter alia, to pay the holder a fixed principal amount on a stated future date and, usually, a series of interest payments during its life.

Bonus issue
A free issue of shares to a company's existing share-holders. No money changes hands and the share price falls pro rata. It is a cosmetic exercise to make the shares more marketable. Also known as a capitalisation or scrip issue.

Book entry transfer
System of recording ownership of securities by computer where the owners do not receive a certificate. Records are kept (and altered) centrally in 'the book'.

Books closed day
Last date for the registration of shares or bonds for the payment of the next.

Borrower's option
See interest rate guarantee.

Bridge
The electronic link enabling transactions between Clearstream and Euroclear participants.

Broker
An agent, often a member of a stock exchange firm or an exchange member himself, who acts as intermediary between buyer and seller. A commission is charged for this service.

Broker/dealer
Firm that operates in dual capacity in the securities marketplace: as principal trading for its own account and as broker representing clients on the market.

Broken date
A maturity date other than the standard ones normally quoted.

Broken period
A period other than the standard ones normally quoted.

Broking
The activity of representing a client as agent and charging commission for doing so.

Bull
Investor who believes prices will rise.

Bull market
A market in which prices are rising, and buyers are more predominant than sellers. Usually refers to equity markets.

Bulldog bonds
A sterling bond issued in London by an overseas government agency. The term is also used for debenture type issues from a commercial organisation.

Buying in
The action taken by a broker failing to receive delivery of securities from a counterparty on settlement date to purchase these securities in the open market.

Calendar spread
The simultaneous purchase (or sale) of a futures or option contract for one date and the sale (or purchase) of a similar futures contract for a different date. See spread.

Call option
An option that gives the seller the right, but not the obligation, to buy a specified quantity of the underlying asset at a fixed price, on or before a specified date. The buyer of a call option has the obligation (because they have bought the right) to make delivery of the underlying asset if the option is exercised by the seller.

Call spread
The purchase of a call option coupled with the sale of another call option at a different strike, expecting a limited rise or fall in the value of the underlying.

Callable bond
A bond that the issuer has the right to redeem prior to maturity by paying some specified call price.

Cap
Also ceiling. A package of interest rate options whereby, at each of a series of future fixing dates, if an agreed reference rate such as LIBOR is higher than the strike rate, the option buyer receives the difference between them, calculated on an agreed notional principal amount for the period until the next fixing date.

Capital adequacy
Requirement for firms conducting investment business to have sufficient funds.

Capital gain (or loss)
Profit (or loss) from the sale of a capital asset. Capital gains may be short term (one year or less) or long term (more than one year). Capital losses are used to offset capital gains to establish a net position for tax purposes.

Capital adequacy rules
Regulations specifying minimum capital requirements for investment businesses and banks.

Capital gains tax (CGT)
Tax payable by individuals on profit made on the disposal of assets.

Capital markets
A term used to describe the means by which large amounts of money (capital) are raised by companies, governments and other organisations for long-term use and the subsequent trading of the instruments issued in recognition of such capital.

Capitalisation issue
See bonus issue.

Carried interest
The general partners' share of the profits generated through a private equity fund, typically 20–25%. Carried interest is designed to be the general partners' chief incentive for strong performance.

The term originated in the early days of venture capital, when general partners put up nothing in return for 20% of the profits; thus the limited partners "carried the interest" of the general partners.

Cash market
Traditionally, this term has been used to denote the market in which commodities were traded for immediate delivery against cash. Since the inception of futures markets for T-bills and other debt securities, a distinction has been made between the cash markets in which these securities trade for immediate delivery and the futures markets in which they trade for future delivery.

Cash sale
A transaction on the London Stock Exchange which calls for delivery of the securities that same day (T0). In "regular way" trades, the seller delivers securities on the third business day (T + 3).

Cash settlement
In the money market, a transaction is said to be made for cash settlement if the securities purchased are delivered against payment on the same day the trade is made.

Ceiling
See cap.

Central bank
Influential institution at the core of a country's monetary and financial system, such as the Bank of England, the Federal Reserve in the USA or the European Central Bank. Its main aim is to ensure price stability in the economy through control of inflation and safeguard the financial industry.

Central Securities Depository (CSD)
An organisation that holds securities in either immobilised or dematerialised form thereby enabling transactions to be processed by book entry transfer. Also provides securities administration services.

Certificate
Paper form of shares (or bonds), representing ownership of a company (or its debt).

Certificate of deposit
A money market instrument in bearer form issued by a bank certifying a deposit made at the bank.

CFD
See contract for difference.

CFTC
The Commodities and Futures Commission (United States).

Chaps
Clearing House Automated Payment System – clearing system for Sterling and Euro payments between banks.

Chapter 11
Area of the US Bankruptcy Reform Act 1978 that protects companies from creditors.

Charts
Graphs used to indicate share price and index movements. Chartists seek to identify from the graphs where selling and support levels are likely to occur and also to establish trend lines that may indicate where fluctuation to the share price is possible.

Cheapest to deliver
The cash security that provides the lowest cost (largest profit) to the arbitrage trader; the cheapest to deliver instrument is used to price the futures contract.

Chinese walls
Artificial barriers to the flow of information set up in large firms to prevent the movement of sensitive information between departments.

CHIPS
Clearing House Interbank Payments System – clearing system for US dollar payments between banks in New York.

Churning
Dealing in a fund's investments more frequently than is reasonable in the circumstances.

City code
Principles and rules written by the panel on takeovers and mergers to regulate conduct during a takeover.

Clean price
The total price of a bond less accrued interest.

Clearance   The process of determining accountability for the exchange of money and securities between counterparties to a trade; clearance creates statements of obligation for securities and/or funds due.

Clearance broker   A broker who will handle the settlement of securities-related transactions for himself or another broker. Sometimes, small brokerage firms may not clear for themselves and therefore employ the services of an outside clearing broker.

Clearing   The centralised process whereby transacted business is recorded and positions are maintained.

Clearing agent   An institution that settles transaction for a large number of counterparties.

Clearing broker   Is the clearing agent for the trading broker in the market where the trade will settle. It is usually the party with which the sub-custodian will actually settle the trade.

Clearing house   Company that acts as central counterparty for the settlement of stock exchange transactions. For example, on TD, broker X sold 100, 300 and 500 securities ABC and purchased 50 and 200 units of the same issue. The clearing system will net the transactions and debit X with 650 units $(-900+250=650)$ against the total cash amount. This enables to reduce the number of movements and thus the costs.

Clearing house funds   Also known as next-day funds, where the proceeds of a trade are available on the day following the actual settlement date.

Clearing organisation   The clearing organisation acts as the guarantor of the performance and settlement of contracts that are traded on an exchange.

Clearing system   System established to clear transactions.

LCH.Clearnet   The clearing house for Euronext, ICE, LME etc.

Clearstream   CSD and clearing house based in Luxembourg and Frankfurt and linked to Deutsche Borse.

Close ended   Organisations such as companies that are a certain size as determined by their share capital.

Closed-end fund	A fund with a fixed number of shares or units where the total number of participants in the fund remains static (see also open-ended fund).
Closed period	A period of time when an investor cannot sell their interest in a fund, e.g. example in a private equity fund this may be the first 5 years
Closing day	In a new bond issue, the day when securities are delivered against payment by syndicate members participating in the offering.
Closing trade	A bought or sold trade which is used to partly offset an open position, to reduce it or to fully offset it and close it.
Cold call	The uninvited contact of potential investors with a view to selling them products. Usually closely regulated to protect the consumer from undue pressure.
Collar	Also cylinder, tunnel, fence or corridor. The sale of a put (or call) option and purchase of a call (or put) at different strikes (typically both out-of-the-money) or the purchase of a cap combined with the sale of a floor.
Collateral	An acceptable asset used to cover a margin requirement.
Collateralised Debt Obligation (CDO)	An instrument made up of a collection of loans, bonds or other debts, packaged and sold as tranches to investors. The lowest tranche bears the highest risk of loss caused by any default until that tranche has been eliminated then the next tranche and so on.
Collateralised mortgage obligations	Bonds backed by a pool of mortgages owned by the issuer. They usually reimburse capital at each coupon payment as per reimbursement of the underlying mortgages.
Collective investment scheme	An investment vehicle that pools together investors money for collective investment examples being mutual funds and unit trusts.
Commercial paper	Short-term obligations with maturities between 2 and 270 days issued by banks, corporations or other borrowers to investors with temporary idle cash. They are usually discounted although some are interest bearing.

Commission	Charge levied by a firm for agency broking.
Commitment	The amount an investor agrees to be committed to providing to a fund and which can be drawn down by the fund as investment opportunities arise.
Commodities	The raw materials traded on specialist markets (see also soft and hard commodities).
Commodity futures	These comprise five main categories: agriculturals wheat and potatoes; softs, for example coffee and cocoa; precious metals, for example gold and silver; non-ferrous metals, for example copper and lead; and energies, for example oil and gas.
Common stock	Securities that represent ownership in a US corporation. The two most important common stockholder rights are the voting right and dividend right. Common stockholder's claims on corporate assets are subordinate to those of bondholders, preferred stockholders and general creditors.
Compliance officer	Person appointed within an authorised firm to be responsible for ensuring compliance with the rules.
Compound annual rate (CAR)	The compounded annual rate of interest on a savings account taking into account the frequency of payment and assuming the re-investment of the interest.
Compound interest	Interest calculated on the assumption that interest amounts will be received periodically and can be re-invested (usually at the same rate).
Conduct of business rules	Rules required by FSA 1986 to dictate how firms conduct their business. They deal mainly with the relationship between firm and client.
Conflicts of interest	Circumstances that arise where a firm has an investment which could encourage it not to treat its clients favourably. The more areas in which a firm is involved the greater the number of potential conflicts.
Confirm	An agreement for each individual OTC transaction which has specific terms.
Consideration	The value of a transaction calculated as the price per share multiplied by the quantity being transferred.

Continuous net settlement	Extends multilateral netting to handle failed trades brought forward – see *multilateral netting*.
Contract	The standard unit of trading for futures and options. It is also commonly referred to as a "lot".
Contract for difference (CFD)	Contract designed to make a profit or avoid a loss by reference to movements in the price of an item. The underlying item cannot change hands.
Contract note	Legal documentation sent by securities house to clients providing details of a transaction completed on their behalf.
Contractual settlement date	Date on which seller and buyer are contractually obligated to settle the securities transaction.
Convergence	The movement of the cash asset price towards the futures price as the expiration date of the futures contract approaches.
Conversion or exchange agent	Similar as for warrant agent, to convert bonds into shares.
Conversion premium	The effective extra cost of buying shares through exercising a convertible bond compared with buying the shares directly in the market. Usually expressed as percentage of the current market price of the shares.
Conversion price	The normal value of a convertible which may be exchanged for one share.
Conversion ratio	The number of shares into which a given amount (e.g. £100 or $1000) of the nominal value of a convertible can be converted.
Convertible bond/ Convertible Securities	Security (usually a bond or preferred stock) that can be exchanged for other securities, usually common stock of the same issuer, at the option of the holder and under certain conditions.
Convertible currency	A currency that is freely convertible into another currency. Currencies for which domestic exchange control legislation specifically allows conversion into other currencies.
Convertible-term assurance	A term assurance policy that can be converted into a whole life or endowment policy.

Cooling-off period	Period of time, usually 7 to 14 days that allows an investor to reconsider and change his or her mind regarding a transaction.
Corporate action	One of many possible capital restructuring changes or similar actions taken by the company, which may have an impact on the market price of its securities, and which may require the shareholders to make certain decisions.
Corporate debt securities	Bonds or commercial papers issued by private corporations.
Corporate finance	General title which covers activities such as raising cash through new issues.
Correlation	Refers to the degree to which fluctuations of one variable are similar to those of another. In funds this can be between the benchmark and the portfolio or the mandated objectives and the actual investments.
Corridor	See collar.
Cornerstone investor	Often the issuer/owner of a fund who subscribes a minimum amount.
Cost of carry	The net running cost of holding a position (which may be negative), e.g., the cost of borrowing cash to buy a bond, less the coupon earned on the bond while holding it.
Counterparty	A trade can take place between two or more counter parties. Usually one party to a trade refers to its trading partners as counterparties.
Coupon	Generally, the nominal annual rate of interest expressed as a percentage of the principal value. The interest is paid to the holder of a fixed income security by the borrower. The coupon is generally paid annually, semi-annually or, in some cases, quarterly depending on the type of security.
Coupon swap	An interest rate swap in which one leg is fixed rate and the other is floating rate. See basis swap.
Covered option	An option bought or sold offsetting an existing underlying position. See naked option.
Credit and charge cards	Means of paying for goods and services without cash. Credit cards normally allow an interest free period

before the account needs to be settled, which can be in full or a minimum monthly payment. Conversely, charge cards although similar in their uses require full repayment.

Credit creation Expansion of loans which in turn expands the money supply.

Credit derivatives Credit derivatives have as the underlying asset some kind of credit default. As with all derivatives, the credit derivative is designed to enable the risk related to a credit issue, such as non-payment of an interest coupon on a corporate or sovereign bond, or the non-repayment of a loan, to be transferred.

Credit risk The risk that a borrower, or counter-party to a deal, or the issuer of a security will default on repayment or not deliver its side of the deal.

CREST The organisation in the UK that holds UK and Irish company shares in dematerialised form and clears and settles trades in UK and Irish company shares. Now merged with Euroclear.

CRESTCo Organisation that owns CREST.

CREST member A participant within CREST who holds stock in stock accounts in CREST and whose name appears on the share register. A member is their own *user*.

Crest-sponsored member A participant within CREST who holds stock in stock accounts in CREST and whose name appears on the share register. Unlike a member, a sponsored member is not their own user. The link to CREST is provided by another user who sponsors the sponsored member.

CREST user A participant within CREST who has an electronic link to CREST.

Cross border trading Trading which takes place between persons or entities from different countries.

Covered writing The sale of call options but the seller owns the stock which would be required to cover the delivery, if called.

Cross currency Interest rate swap An interest rate swap where the interest payments are in two different currencies and the exchange rate, for the final settlement, is agreed at the outset of the transaction.

Cum-dividend	With dividend.
Cum rights	A term applied to a stock trading in the market-place "with subscription rights attached" which is reflected in the price of that security.
Cumulative dividend	Dividend that is due but not yet paid on cumulative preferred shares. These must be paid before any ordinary dividends are paid.
Cumulative preference share	If the company fails to pay a preference dividend, the entitlement to the dividend accumulates and the arrears of preference dividend must be paid before any ordinary dividend.
Currency exposure	Currency exposure exists if assets are held or income earned in one currency while liabilities are denominated in another currency. The position is exposed to changes in the relative values of the two currencies such that the cost of the liabilities may be increased or the value of the assets or earning decreased.
Currency futures	Contracts calling for delivery of a specific amount of a foreign currency at a specified future date in return for a given amount of, say, US dollars.
Currency swap	An agreement to exchange interest-related payments in the same currency from fixed rate into floating rate (or vice versa) or from one type of floating rate to another. A currency swap is different to an interest rate swap as the principal amounts are also swapped.
Current account	Account that allows deposits and payments usually via cheque book.
CUSIP	The committee on Uniform Securities Identification Procedures, the body which established a consistent securities numbering system in the United States.
CUSIP Number	Unique nine-digit number that identifies securities, US or non-US, which trade and settle in the United States (Committee on Uniform Security Identification Procedure).
Custodian	Institution holding securities in safekeeping for a client. A custodian also offers different services to its clients (settlement, portfolio services etc.).

Customer – non-private	Customer who is assumed to understand the workings of the investment world and therefore receives little protection from the FSA Conduct of Business Rules.
Customer – private	Customer who is assumed to be financially unsophisticated and therefore receives more protection from the FSA Conduct of Business Rules.
Cylinder	See collar.
Daily cash sweep	The action of investing a client's cash balance that would otherwise lie idle overnight, in an interest bearing deposit or investment vehicle. Generally performed on an overnight basis.
Daily official list	London Stock Exchange produced document which provides record of prices at which all stocks were traded on the previous day.
Day count fraction	The proportion of a year by which an interest rate is multiplied in order to calculate the amount accrued or payable.
Day-light exposure	The risk to the deliverer of securities or payer of countervalue to the possibility of a counterparty defaulting on his obligations during the business day.
Dealer	Individual or firm that acts as principal in all transactions, buying for his own account.
Debenture	Another name for a corporate bond – usually secured on assets of the company.
Default	Failure to perform on a contract, either cash settlement or physical settlement, e.g. an investor failing to pay for shares applied for in a fund or a manager failing to settle obligations with a broker or vice versa.
Deferred annuity	An annuity which first becomes payable at a future date.
Deferred share	A class of share where the holder is only entitled to a dividend if the ordinary shareholders have been paid a specified minimum dividend.
Definitive bond	Any bond issued in final form. It is used particularly in reference to permanent bonds for which Temporary Bonds or Interim Certificates were issued.

Deliverable basket	The list of securities that meets the delivery standards of futures contracts.
Delivery	The physical movement of the underlying asset on which the derivative is based from seller to buyer.
Delivery versus payment	Settlement where transfer of the security and payment for that security occur simultaneously. Also known as DVP.
Delta	The sensitivity of an option price to changes in the price of the underlying product.
Dematerialised (form)	Circumstances where securities are held in a book entry transfer system with no certificates.
Depositary	An authorised firm that is responsible for safe custody of a funds assets and oversight of the associate corporate director/investment manager, similar role to a Trustee.
Depository receipts	Certificate issued by a bank in a country to represent shares of a foreign corporation issued in a foreign country. It entitles the holder to dividends and capital gains. They trade and pay dividend in the currency of the country of issuance of the certificate.
Depository Trust Company (DTC)	A US central securities depository through which members may arrange deliveries of securities between each other through electronic debit and credit entries without the physical delivery of the securities. DTC is industry owned with the NYSE as the majority owner. DTC is a member of the Federal Reserve System.
Depreciation	The erosion of the value of something caused by a reduction in the value of a currency influenced by, for example, inflation and also the declining value created by a second hand sale of those goods, e.g. a motor car.
Derivative	A financial instrument whose value is dependent upon the value of an underlying asset.
Derivative instruments or derivative securities	Securities which are based on other underlying securities, e.g. options or futures. Derivative securities do not create wealth, rather they provide for the transfer of risk from hedgers to speculators.

Dilution   Reducing the actual or potential earnings per share by issuing more shares or giving options to obtain them.

Dilution levy   A fee charged to a buyer or seller of shares or units in a fund to adjust any discrepancy in value caused by using a mid-price in calculating the NAV per share.

Direct debit   A method of payment where, on a regular basis, funds are extracted from the payer's account and paid into the recipient's account. A direct debit is variable and as such the amount debited can change.

Direct market participant   A broker, broker/dealer or any direct member of an exchange.

Direct placement   Selling a new issue by placing it with one or several institutional investors rather than offering it for sale publicly.

Dirty price   The total price of a bond including accrued interest.

Disclaimer   A notice or statement intending to limit or avoid potential legal liability.

Discount   The amount by which an instrument or fund is priced below its theoretical price/value.

Discount factor   The number by which a future cash flow must be multiplied in order to calculate its present value.

Discount rate   The rate of interest charged by the Federal Reserve in the US to banks to whom money has been lent. Is also a term used by other central banks for the same purpose.

Discount securities Non-interest bearing, short-term securities that are issued at discount and redeemed at maturity for full face value.

Discretionary trust A trust where the trustees have discretion as to the distribution of the income and capital of the trust.

Distribution   The payment of income, interest or assets in respect of the investors entitlement.

Distribution shares or units   Shares or units in a fund where the income is distributed to the investor.

Dividend	Distribution of profits made by a company to its shareholders if it chooses to do so.
Dividend cover	Dividends are paid out of a company's profits and dividend cover is the excess profits after the dividend has been calculated. For example, if a company has a profit of £60,000 and the total dividend is £10,000, the dividend is covered six times.
Dividend per share	Indicated annual dividend based on the most recently announced quarterly dividend times four plus any additional dividends to be paid during the current fiscal year.
Dividend yield	The dividend expressed as a percentage of the share price.
Diversification	Investment strategy of spreading risk by investing the total available in a range of investments.
Domestic bond	Bond issued in the country of the issuer, in its country and according to the regulations of that country.
Domicile	Where an individual, fund or a business is legally deemed to be registered, based or living.
Double taxation treaty	An agreement between two countries intended to avoid or limit the double taxation of income. Under the terms of the treaty an investor with tax liabilities in both countries can either apply for a reduction of taxed imposed by one country or credit taxes paid in that country against tax liabilities in the other.
Dow Jones index	Main share index used in the USA and used as a benchmark for US equity funds.
Down-and-out option	A knock-out option where the trigger is lower than the underlying rate at the start. See up-and-in option, down-and-in option, up-and-out option.
Drop-lock	A hybrid form of floating rate note that converts into a fixed-rate bond once interest rates drop to a predetermined level.
DRP or (DRIP)	Dividend reinvestment plan.
DTC	Depository Trust Company – CSD for shares in the USA.
Due diligence	The carrying out of duties with care and perseverance. Due diligence is generally referred to in

connection with the investigations of a company, carried out by accountants to ascertain the value of that company and also applies from a regulatory point of view that firms and key personnel should carry out their duties with due diligence to the regulatory environment.

Duration   A measure of the relative volatility of a bond; it is an approximation for the price change of a bond for a given change in the interest rate. Duration is measured in units of time. It includes the effects of time until maturity, cash flows and the yield to maturity.

Dutch auction   A Dutch auction is where bids are made by an open outcry or electronic system method and are accepted in descending order until the issue is completed.

EFP   Exchange of futures for physical. Common in the energy markets. A physical deal priced on the futures markets, with the derivative transacted off exchange but recognised by the exchange for clearing.

Earnings per share (EPS)   The total profit of a company divided by the number of shares in issue.

Effective date   The date on which the interest period to which a FRA or swap relates is to start.

Elective event   Corporate action that requires a choice from the security owner.

Electronic order book   The electronic order matching system used as the system for dealing in the shares that comprise the FT-SE 100 stock.

Embedded option   An option which is included as part of a product.

Emerging market   Non-industrialised country with

- low or middle per capita income, as published annually by the World Bank
- undeveloped capital market (i.e. the market represents only a small portion of their GDP).

Endowment policy   Form of saving linked with life assurance. Must be held for at least 10 years to get full benefit.

Equilisation Method of ensuring a fair and equitable share amongst investors of performance fees in a hedge fund. Also used in unit trusts to balance the amount of dividend distributed between actual income earned and that paid for in the price when buying the unit.

Equity A common term to describe stocks or shares.

Equity/stock options Contracts based on individual equities or shares. On exercise of the option the specified amount of shares are exchanged between the buyer and the seller through the clearing organisation.

Equity index swap An obligation between two parties to exchange cash flows based on the percentage change in one or more stock indices, for a specific period with previously agreed re-set dates. The swap is cash settled and based on notional principal amounts. One side of an equity swap can involve a LIBOR reference rate.

Equity "kicker" Often allied to mezzanine debt it offers an equity opportunity such as a warrant as an incentive to the investor.

ERISA The Employee Retirement Income Security Act (1974) established to protect participants and beneficiaries in employee benefit/retirement plans.

Escrow A bank account specifically designed to hold money during a dispute between two or more parties to prevent access to those funds until finalised.

E-T-D This is the common term which is used to describe exchange-traded derivatives which are the standardised products. It also differentiates products which are listed on an exchange as opposed to those offered over-the-counter.

ETF Exchange-traded funds Passively managed basket of stocks that mirrors a particular index and that can be traded like ordinary shares. They trade intraday on stock exchanges, like securities, at market-determined prices. In essence, ETFs are index funds that trade like stocks.

Ethical investments The investment in specific sectors through either personal conviction or the view that such companies have a higher potential, e.g. investment in funds or companies supporting 'green' issues, or the

	avoidance of so-called 'unethical' areas such as animal experimentation, pollution etc.
EUCLID	The Euroclear electronic communication system.
EURIBOR	A measure of the average cost of funds over the whole euro area based on a panel of 57 banks.
Euro	The name of the single European currency.
Euro-commercial paper	Unsecured corporate debt with a short maturity structured to appeal to large financial institutions active in the Euro market.
Eurobond	An interest bearing security issued across national borders, usually issued in a currency other than that of the issuer's home country. Because there is no regulatory protection, only governments and top-rated multinational corporations can issue Eurobonds that the market will accept.
Euroclear	A book-entry clearing facility for most Eurocurrency and foreign securities. Linked to Euronext through the acquisition of SICOVAM, and has recently announced a merger with CREST.
European Bank for Reconstruction and Development	An institution established to provide financial assistance to Eastern Europe.
European Investment Bank	Set up by the European Union and funded by member states to provide aid in areas of unemployment and poverty and also assists with industrial projects.
European Monetary System (EMS)	Agreement between most members of the common market on how to organise their currencies.
European style option	An option which can be exercised only on the expiry day.
Exception-based processing	Transaction processing where straightforward items are processed automatically, allowing staff to concentrate on the items which are incorrect or not straightforward.
Exceptional	In accounting, unexpected or one-off losses and gains are known as exceptional. They are part

of a company's pre-tax profit and although irregular they are derived from the company's normal business.

Execution and clearing agreement An agreement signed between the client and the clearing broker. This agreement sets out the terms by which the clearing broker will conduct business with the client.

Exchange Market place for trading.

Exchange delivery settlement price (EDSP) The price determined by the exchange for physical delivery of the underlying instrument or cash settlement.

Exchange-owned clearing organisation Exchange- or member-owned clearing organisations are structured so that the clearing members guarantee each other with the use of a members default fund and additional funding like insurance with no independent guarantee.

Exchange rate The rate at which one currency can be exchanged for another.

Exchange rate mechanism That part of the EMS that relates to pegging the rates against each other within predetermined limits.

Excise duties Taxes on alcohol, tobacco and hydrocarbons.

Ex-date Date on or after which a sale of securities is executed without the right to receive dividends or other entitlements.

Ex-dividend Gilt-edged stocks are made 'ex-dividend' 37 days before interest payment is due. After a stock has become 'ex-dividend', a buyer of stock purchases it without the right to receive the next (pending) interest payment.

Execute and eliminate order Type of order input into SETS. The amount that can be tracked immediately against displayed orders is completed, with the remainder being rejected.

Execution The action of trading in the markets.

Execution and clearing agreement An agreement signed between the client and the clearing broker. This agreement sets out the terms by which the clearing broker will conduct business with the client.

Execution only or give-up Agreement	Tri-partite agreements that are signed by the executing broker, the clearing broker and the client. This agreement sets out the terms by which the clearing broker will accept business on behalf of the client.
Exercise	The process by which the holder of an option may take up their right to buy or sell the underlying asset.
Exercise price (or strike price)	The fixed price, per share or unit, at which an option conveys the right to call (purchase) or put (sell) the underlying shares or units.
Exit fee	Charge levied on an investor if they exits from a fund in the early (typically 5 years) years of ownership.
Exotic options	New generation of option derivatives, including look-backs, barriers, baskets, ladders etc. They have different terms to standardised traded options.
Expenses	The fund's costs incurred in buying and selling shares. Also included are costs associated with sales, marketing, client services, legal expertise etc.
Expiry date	The last date on which an option holder can exercise their right. After this date an option is deemed to lapse or be abandoned.
Extraordinary general meeting (EGM)	Any meeting of an investment company's shareholders other than its AGM.
Ex-warrants	Trading a security so that the buyer will not be entitled to warrants that will be distributed to holders.
Face value	The value of a bond, note, mortgage or other security that appears on the face of the issue, unless the value is otherwise specified by the issuing company. Face value is ordinarily the amount the issuing company promises to pay at maturity. Face value is also referred to as par value or nominal value.
Failed transaction	A securities transaction that does not settle on time, i.e. the securities and/or cash are not exchanged as agreed on the settlement date.

Fair value

For futures, it is the true price not the market price, allowing for the cost of carry. For options, it is the true price not the market price, as calculated using an option pricing model.

Federal reserve book entry system

CSD for US government securities.

Fill or kill order

Type of order input into SETS. It is either completed in full against displayed orders or rejected in full.

Final salary pension

Company pension that provides benefits dependent on salary in the final years prior to retirement and the number of years in the scheme. A number of variations are available; the most common being a 60th scheme. To gain maximum benefit, the member would have to be in the scheme for 40 years. The benefits payable would be two-thirds of final salary as defined by the scheme (40/60ths).

Final settlement

The completion of a transaction when the delivery of all components of a trade is performed.

Financial futures/options contracts

Financial futures is a term used to describe futures contracts based on financial instruments like currencies, debt instruments and financial indices.

Financial Services and Markets Act 2000

The legislation that created the single UK regulator, the Financial Services Authority.

Financial services authority (FSA)

The agency designated by the UK Treasury to regulate investment business as required by FSA 1986. It is the main regulator of the financial sector and was formerly called the Securities and Investments Board (SIB). It assumed its full powers on 1 December 2001.

First notice day

The first day that the holders of short positions can give notification to the exchange/clearing house that they wish to effect delivery.

Fiscal agent

A commercial bank appointed by the borrower to undertake certain duties related to the new issue,

	such as assisting the payment of interest and principal, redeeming bonds or coupons, handling taxes, replacement of lost or damaged securities, destruction of coupons and bonds once payments have been made.
Fiscal policy	Policy laid down by the Treasury to take into account taxation, spending, borrowing etc. and the effect it has on the economy.
Fiscal years	These run from 6 April to 5 April and are the periods of assessment for both income tax and capital gains tax.
Fit and proper	Under FSA 86 everyone conducting investment business must be a 'fit and proper person'. The Act does not define the term, a function which is left to the regulators such as FSA.
Fixed income	Interest on a security that is calculated as a constant specified percentage of the principal amount and paid at the end of specified interest periods, usually annually or semi-annually, until maturity.
Fixed leg	In a coupon swap, the flow of a fixed-rate interest payment from one party to the other.
Fixed rate	A borrowing or investment where the interest or coupon paid is fixed throughout the arrangement.
Fixed rate cont'd	In a FRA or coupon swap, the fixed rate is the fixed interest rate paid by one party to the other, in return for a floating rate receipt (i.e. an interest rate that is to be re-fixed at some future time or times).
Fixed-rate borrowing	A fixed rate borrowing establishing the interest rate that will be paid throughout the life of the loan.
Fixed-rate payer	In a coupon swap, the party that pays the fixed rate.
Fixed-rate receiver	In a coupon swap, the party that receives the fixed rate.
Flat position	A position which has been fully closed out and no liability to make or take delivery exists.
Flat yield	The yield of a bond calculated as

$$\frac{\text{Annual Coupon}}{\text{Current market price}} \times 100\%$$

Also called the income yield.

Flex options Newly introduced contracts which are a cross between OTCs and exchange-traded products. The advantage of flex options is that participants can choose various parts of the contract specification such as the expiry date and exercise price.

Flotation When a company has its shares first quoted on the stock market it is said to have 'floated' its shares.

Floating leg In a coupon swap, the flow of a floating-rate interest payment from one party to the other.

Floating rate A borrowing or investment where the interest or coupon paid changes throughout the arrangement in line with some reference rate such as LIBOR.

Floating rate cont'd In a FRA or coupon swap, the floating rate is the floating interest rate (i.e. an interest rate that is to be re-fixed at some future time or times) paid by one party to the other, in return for a fixed-rate receipt.

Floating rate note (FRN) Bond where each interest payment is made at the current or average market levels, often by reference to LIBOR.

Floating rate payer Same as fixed rate received in a coupon swap.

Floating rate receiver Same as fixed-rate payer in a coupon swap.

Floor A package of interest rate options whereby, at each of a series of future fixing dates, if an agreed reference rate such as LIBOR is lower that the strike rate, the option buyer received the difference between them, calculated on an agreed notional principal amount for the period until the next fixing date. See cap, collar.

Floorbrokerage The process of delegating the execution of futures and options to another counterparty.

Foreign bond Bond issued in a domestic market in the domestic currency and under the domestic rules of issuance by a foreign issuer (e.g. Samurai bonds are bonds issued by issuers of other countries on the Japanese market).

Foreign currency fund A mutual fund investing in foreign currencies.

Foreign exchange	Exchange of one currency into another one.
Forex	Abbreviation for foreign exchange (currency trading).
Forward market	Where a price is agreed now for delivery of goods in the future. Used in currency, securities and commodities markets, often in conjunction with dealing in immediate delivery (see spot market) as a safety net.
Forward pricing	A UK term for unit trusts that are bought and sold at the next valuation price.
Forward rate agreements (FRAs)	An agreement where the client can fix the rate of interest that will be applied to a notional loan or deposit, drawn or placed on an agreed date in the future, for a specified term.
Forward delivery	Transactions which involve a delivery date in the future.
Forwardation	Where a dealer purchases goods on the spot market to meet his future obligations, especially when those goods are cheaper now than quoted on the forward market.
Forwards	Are very similar to futures contracts but they are not mainly traded on an exchange. They are not marked to market daily but settled only on the delivery date.
Franked income	Where tax has already been paid on income.
Free of payment	Refers to the buying and selling of foreign currencies where there is no associated countervalue or is not dependent on the simultaneous payment of the cash countervalue during the movement of assets.
Friendly society	Societies formed initially to benefit members in return for regular contributions against sickness, poverty and bereavement. Now generally provide various insurance covers (life, medical etc.) as well as savings vehicles.
Front end loading	The deduction of costs (commission, administration, etc.) from the initial contributions to savings vehicles such as unit trusts, endowment policies or personal pension plans.

Front running	The illicit utilizing by brokers and market makers of advance warning or information for personal or corporate profit.
FSA	Financial Services Authority UK – Financial Services Agency (Japan).
FT Index	The Financial Times Ordinary Share Index consists of 30 large companies across a broad field and gives an indication of share price trends. The larger index, the FT-SE 100 (Footsie), provides a wider indication of 100 leading companies on the stock market. All stock markets have an index, e.g. The Dow Jones in the US, the DAX in Germany or the Nikkei in Japan.
FT-SE 100 index	Main UK share index based on 100 leading shares.
FT-SE Mid 250	UK share index based on the 250 shares immediately below the top 100.
Fund administrator	A firm that provides services to the fund covering areas such as pricing and NAV calculation, performance fee calculation, equilisation, transfer agency etc.
Fund manager	Individuals or specialists companies responsible for investing the assets of a fund in such a way as to maximise its value. They do this by following a strategy to buy and sell equities and other financial instruments.
Fund of funds	A fund that invests only in other funds; can also be a fund of hedge funds that only invests in other hedge funds.
FundSettle	System operated by Euroclear for settlement of investment funds.
Fungibility	A futures contract with identical administration in more than one financial centre. Trades in various geographical locations can be off-set. (e.g. bought on the IPE and sold on the SIMEX).
Futures	An agreement to buy or sell an asset at a certain time in the future for a certain price.
Future value	The amount of money which can be achieved at a given date in the future by investing (or borrowing) a given sum of money now at a given interest rate,

	assuming compound re-investment (or re-funding) of any interest payments received (or paid) before the end.
Futures and options fund (FOF)	Type of authorised unit trust that can invest partially in derivatives.
Geared futures and options fund (GFOF)	Type of authorised unit trust that can invest in derivatives.
Gearing	The characteristic of derivatives which enables a far greater reward for the same, or much smaller, initial outlay. It is the ratio of exposure to investment outlay, and is also known as leverage.
General partner	Partner in a limited liability company or partnership who is the investment manager.
General principles	Eleven fundamental principles of behaviour written by FSA to apply to all investment businesses.
Generic	A generic swap is one for a standard period, against a standard fixing benchmark such as LIBOR.
Gilt	Domestic sterling-denominated, long-term bond backed by the full faith and credit of the United Kingdom and issued by the Treasury.
Gilt-edged market makers (GEMMs)	A firm that is a market maker in gilts. Also known as a primary dealer.
Gilt-edged security	UK government borrowing.
Give-up	The process of giving a trade to a third party who will undertake the clearing and settlement of the trade.
Global bond	A (temporary) certificate representing the whole of a bond issue.
Global certificate	Certificate held at the Central Depository recording the total issue of a bond.
Global clearing	The channelling of the settlement of all futures and options trades through a single counterparty or through a number of counterparties geographically located.

Global custodian	Institution that safekeeps, settles and performs processing of income collection, tax reclaim, multi-currency reporting, cash management, foreign exchange, corporate action and proxy monitoring etc. for clients' securities in all required marketplaces.
Global depository receipt (GDR)	A security representing shares held in custody in the country of issue.
Global system of tax	A tax system whereby the residents of a country are taxed on their worldwide income.
Gold	Widely used commodity and regarded as a safe haven in times of uncertainty.
Good delivery	Proper delivery of certificates that are negotiable and complete in terms of documentation or information.
Grey market	Generally, the market for a new issue before the securities have been distributed to subscribers.
Gross	A position which is held with both the bought and sold trades kept open.
Gross domestic product (GDP)	A measure of the country's entire output.
Gross redemption yield (GRY)	The annual return on owning a bond, allowing both for interest and profit on redemption.
Grossing up	The process of calculating the gross income from a figure net of taxation.
Group	Where one company controls one or more other companies, they are collectively a group.
Group of ten (G10)	Comprising the US, Germany, France, Italy, the Netherlands, Belgium, Sweden, Canada, Japan and Britain. Representatives of G10, as it is known, are made up of finance ministers and treasury officials and meet when necessary to provide support and take action.
Group of thirty (G30)	Private international organisation aiming to deepen understanding of international economic and financial issues. Established in 1978, it is a private, non-profit international body composed of very senior

representatives of the private and public sectors and academia.

Growth stock Companies with or with the expectation of a rapid rise in expansion and subsequent share value.

GSCC Government Securities Clearing Corporation – clearing organisation for US Treasury securities.

Guaranteed annuity An annuity which is payable for a minimum period regardless of whether the annuitant survives.

Guaranteed bond Bonds on which the principal or income or both are guaranteed by another corporation or parent company in case of default by the issuing corporation.

Haircut Securities industry term referring to formulas used in the valuation of securities for the purpose of calculating a broker-dealer's net capital. Also called margin.

Hard commodities Commodities such as tin or zinc. Futures on them are traded on the London Metal Exchange.

Hedge fund A fund that is subject to less regulation than other mutual funds and is able to use many strategies to generate performance. Because of the possible greater risk, most hedge funds cannot be sold or marketed to the public and are sold instead to qualifying investors and institutional investors.

Hedge ratio Determining the ratio of the futures to the cash position so as to reduce price risk.

Hedging A trading method which is designed to reduce or mitigate risk. Reducing the risk of a cash position in the futures instrument to offset the price movement of the cash asset. A broader definition of hedging includes using futures as a temporary substitute for the cash position.

Historic pricing A UK term for units bought or sold at the last valuation price

Holder A person who has bought an open derivatives contract.

Holder of record The party whose name appears on a company's stockholder register at the close of business on record date. That party will receive a dividend or other distribution from the company in the near future.

Holding company	A company which owns more than 50% of the shares of another company as its holding company.
Home state regulation	Under the ISD, an investment business is authorised in the place of its head office and registered office. This home state authorisation entitles it to conduct business in any member state of the European Union.
Host state regulation	Any European investment business operating outside its home basis is regulated by its host for its conduct of business.
ICOM	International Currency Options Market standard documentation for netting foreign exchange option settlements.
ICSD	The International Central Securities Depository. Clears and settles international securities or cross-border transactions through local CSDs.
Immediate annuity	An annuity which is payable as soon as the lump sum has been invested.
Immobilisation	The storage of securities certificates in a vault in order to eliminate physical movement of certificates/documents in transfer of ownership.
Implied repo rate	The rate of return before financing costs implied by a transaction where a longer-term cash security is purchased and a futures contract is sold (or vice versa).
In-the-money	A call option where the exercise price is below the underlying share price or a put option where the exercise price is above the underlying share price.
Income tax	An annual tax on the income of an individual.
Independent clearing organisation	The independent organisation is quite separate from the actual members of the exchange, and will guarantee to each member the performance of the contracts by having them registered in the organisation's name.
Indexation	Where investments, wages, contributions and so on are linked to a benchmark such as inflation. For example, a contribution to a pension scheme may increase by 3% or the retail price index, whichever is the higher.

Individual savings account	ISAs replaced PEPs and TESSAs. A tax-free investment with limitations where the individual can save either on a regular monthly or on lump sum basis with exposure to varying degrees of risk. An ISA is a 'wrapper' into which cash, unit trust and mutual funds are placed.
Inflation	A period of generally rising prices and devaluation of money through a number of causes such as rises in fuel, manufacturing and labour costs. For example, high salary or wage demands not covered by productivity.
Inflation accounting	The allowing for the impact of inflation in preparing company accounts.
Index funds	Unit trusts which invest in the constituent parts of an index.
Index linked bond	Bond whose interest payment and redemption value are linked to the retail prices index.
Index swap	Sometimes the same as a basis swap. Otherwise, a swap where payments on one or both of the legs are based on the value of an index, such as an equity index.
Indirect market participation	Non-broker/dealers, such as institutional investors, who are active investors/traders.
Inheritance tax	A tax charged on the chargeable estate (or wealth) of a deceased person.
Initial fee	Fee charged to the investor when buying into a fund, sometimes called a " front load".
Initial margin	The deposit that the clearing house calls as protection against a default of a contract. It is returnable to the clearing member once the position is closed. The level is subject to changes in line with market conditions.
Inland revenue	The government department responsible for the administration and collection of tax in the UK.
Inside information	Information relating to a security which is not publicly known and which would affect the price of the security if it were public.
Insider	Directors, employees, shareholders and other persons having inside information.

Insider dealing	The criminal offence whereby those with unpublished price sensitive information deal advise others to deal or pass the information on. Maximum penalty is 7-year jail sentence and an unlimited fine.
Institutional investor	An institution which is usually investing money on behalf of others. Examples are mutual funds and pension funds.
Integration	The third stage of money laundering in which the money is finally integrated into the legitimate economy. See placement, layering.
Interbank market	A market for transactions exclusively or predominantly within the banking system. In most countries, the market for short-term money is an Interbank market since banks borrow and lend among one and another in order to balance their books on a daily basis. Non-bank entities may or may not be permitted to participate.
Interbank rates	The bid and offered rates at which international banks place deposits with each other.
Inter dealer broker (IDB)	Member of the London Stock Exchange that acts as a link between firms to enable them to trade with each other anonymously.
Interest rate futures	Based on a debt instrument such as a Government Bond or a Treasury Bill as the underlying product and require the delivery of a bond or bill to fulfil the contract.
Interest rate cap	An option product where the holder (buyer) is guaranteed a maximum borrowing cost over a specified term at a rate of his choosing. A premium is required.
Interest rate collar	An option product where the holder (buyer) is guaranteed a maximum and minimum borrowing cost over a specified term at rates of his choosing. A premium may be required, but may net to zero. Involves the simultaneous trading of caps and floors.
Interest rate floor	An option product where the holder (buyer) is guaranteed a minimum yield on a deposit over a specified term at a rate of his choosing. A premium is required.

Interest rate guarantee	Also IRG. Effectively an option on a forward rate agreement. An IRG can be either a borrower's option (i.e. a call on an FRAO) or a lender's option (i.e. a put on an FRA).
Interest rate swap	An agreement to exchange interest-related payments in the same currency from fixed rate into floating rate (or vice versa) or from one type of floating rate to another.
Interim dividend	Dividend paid part way through a year in advance of the final dividend.
International depository receipt (IDR)	Receipt of shares of a foreign corporation held in the vaults of a depository bank. The receipt entitles the holder to all dividends and capital gains. Dividends and capital gains are converted to local currency as part of the service. IDRs allow investors to purchase foreign shares without having to involve themselves in foreign settlements and currency conversion.
International equity	An equity of a company based outside the UK but traded internationally.
International financial centre	A territory with very low tax rates which also offers international banking, investment and other financial services.
International Monetary Fund	Set up by the Bretton Woods agreement into which member countries contribute to provide assistance during periods of economic instability, thereby smoothing out the world trade cycle and avoiding a major plunge into depression as seen in the 1930s.
International Petroleum Exchange (IPE)	London market for derivatives of petrol and oil products, now part of the Intercontinental Exchange.
International Standards Organisation (ISO)	An international federation of organisations of various industries which seeks to set common international standards in a variety of fields.
International securities identification (ISIN)	A coding system developed by the ISO for identifying securities. ISINs are designated to create one unique worldwide number for any security. It is a 12 digit alpha/numeric code.

Interpolation	The estimation of a price or rate, usually for a broken date, from two other rates or prices, each of which is for a date either side of the required date.
In-the-money	An option whose strike is more advantageous to the option buyer than the current market rate. See at-the-money, out-of-the-money.
Intervention	The process whereby the Bank of England acts to influence the exchange rate for sterling by buying it to support its value or selling it to weaken it.
Intra-day margin	An extra margin call which the clearing organisation can call during the day when there is a very large movement up or down in the price of the contract.
Intrinsic value	The amount by which an option is in-the-money.
IRG	See interest rate guarantee.
IRS	See interest rate swap.
Investment banks	A bank that has multiple activities, that is banking, principal trading, asset management etc.
Investment company with variable capital ICVC	A term for an open-ended investment company used in Europe similar to OEIC (UK) or mutual fund (US).
Investment Services Directive (ISD)	European Union Directive imposing common standards on investment business.
Investment trust company	Company whose sole business consists of buying, selling and holding shares. The difference with unit trusts is that investors in unit trusts do not receive a part of the profits of the company managing the trust.
Investor protection committee (IPC)	Divisions of the ABI and NAPF set up to monitor their positions as shareholders.
Investment business	Dealing, advising or managing investments. Those doing so need to be authorised.
Investments	Items defined by the regulator to be regulated by it. Can include shares, bonds, options, futures, life assurance and pensions.

Investment grade A grading level that is used by certain types of funds for determining assets that are suitable for investment in by the fund.

Investment trust (company) A company whose sole function is to invest in the shares of other companies.

Invoice amount The amount calculated under the formula specified by the futures exchange, which will be paid in settlement of the delivery of the underlying asset.

IOSCO International Organisation of Securities Commissions.

IPMA International Primary Markets Association.

Irredeemable gilt A gilt with no fixed date for redemption. Investors receive interest indefinitely.

ISDA International Swaps and Derivatives Association, previously known as the International Swap Dealers Association. Many market participants use ISDA documentation.

ICMA/ISMA International Capital Market Association/ International Securities Markets Association.

ISSA The International Securities Services Association.

Issue Stocks or bonds sold by a corporation or government entity at a particular time.

Issue price The percentage of principal value at which the price of a new issue of securities is fixed.

Issuer Legal entity that issues and distributes securities.

Issuing agent Agent (e.g. bank) who puts original issues out for sale.

Issuing house Institutions that issue shares for companies wishing to raise capital by underwriting shares issued direct to the public through the company or by buying and selling the shares itself.

JSE Johannesburg Stock Exchange.

Junk bonds High risk bonds that have low ratings or are in default, where there is a risk of non-payment of obligations such as interest or bond redemption. Also known as high yield bonds.

Knock-in-option	An option which is activated if a trigger level is reached. See barrier option, knock-out option.
Knock-out option	An option which is cancelled if a trigger level is reached. See barrier option, knock-in option.
Know your customer	The conduct of business rule requiring investment advisers to take steps, before giving investment advice, to determine the financial position and investment objectives of the client.
Last notice day	The final day that notification of delivery of a futures contract will be possible. On most exchanges all outstanding short futures contracts will be automatically delivered to open long positions.
Last trading day	Often the day preceding last notice day which is the final opportunity for holders of long positions to trade out of their positions and avoid ultimate delivery.
Layering	The second stage of money laundering, in which the money is passed through a series of transaction to obscure its origin. See placement, integration.
LCH.Clearnet	The now merged London Clearing House and Clearnet.
Lead managers	In the eurobond markets, the description given to the securities house appointed to handle a new issue.
Legal title or ownership	Legal title to property is held by the person who controls the property and in whose name the property is registered.
Level-term assurance	A term assurance policy where the sum assured remains constant (or level) throughout the term.
Leverage	The magnification of gains and losses by only paying for part of the underlying value of the instrument or asset; the smaller the amount of funds invested, the greater the leverage. It is also known as gearing.
Leveraged buyout	A leveraged buyout (or LBO, or highly-leveraged transaction, (HLT) occurs when a financial sponsor gains control of a majority of a target company's equity through the use of borrowed money or debt.

LIBID   The London inter-bank bid rate. The rate at which one bank will lend to another.

LIBOR   The London inter-bank offered rate. It is the rate used when one bank borrows from another bank. It is the benchmark used to price many capital market and derivative transactions.

Life assurance policy   A contract between an insurance company (the life office) and an individual or individuals, where payment by the life office in return for premiums paid depends in some way on the duration of a human life or lives often linked to investment, that is a life fund.

Life interest   The interest of the life tenant in a trust.

Life of another policy   Life assurance policy taken out on the life of another person.

Life office   Another name for a life assurance company.

LIFFE   London International Financial Futures and Options Exchange, now part of Euronext.

Limited partner   Partner in a limited liability company or partnership who subscribes funds but has no say in the investments of the portfolio.

Limit order   Type of order input into SETS. If not completed immediately, the balance is displayed on the screen and forms the Order Book.

Limit order cont'd   An order in which a customer sets the maximum price he is willing to pay as a buyer or the minimum price he is willing to accept as a seller.

Line of credit   A commitment by a bank or prime broker to make loans to a borrower like a hedge fund up to a specified maximum during a specified period.

Linked Forex   When the currency contract is purchased to cover the local cost of a security trade.

Liquidator   Person appointed to sell the corporate assets of a company in receivership, distributing the proceeds among its creditors.

Liquidity   A liquid asset is one that can be converted easily and rapidly into cash without a substantial loss of value. In the money market, a security is said to be liquid if the spread between bid and asked

	price is narrow and reasonable size can be done at those quotes.
Liquidity risk	The risk that a bank may not be able to close out a position because the market is illiquid.
Listed company	Company which has been admitted to listing on a stock exchange and whose shares can then be dealt on that exchange.
Listed securities	Securities listed on a stock exchange are tradeable on this exchange.
Listing	Status applied for by companies whose securities are then listed on the London Stock Exchange and available to be traded.
Listing particulars	Detailed information that must be published by a company applying to be listed.
Listing rules	Rule book for listed companies which governs their behaviour. Commonly known as the Yellow Book.
Lloyds of London	World's largest insurance market.
Load	A term used to describe a fee paid by an investor, i.e. that is front end load, back end load, no load – UK term is initial fee, exit fee etc.
Loan stock	See *bonds*.
Local	An individual member of an exchange who trades solely for their own account.
Local currency	Currency of the country of settlement.
Lombard rate	The rate of interest at which the German Bundesbank lends to commercial banks when the loans are against treasury bills or bills of exchange.
London inter bank offer rate (LIBOR)	Rate at which banks lend to each other which is often used as the benchmark for floating rate loans (FRNs).
London International Financial Futures and Options Exchange (LIFFE)	Market for trading in bond, interest rate, FT-SE 100 index and FT-SE Mid 250 index, futures, plus equity options and soft commodity derivatives, now part of Euronext.
London Metal Exchange (LME)	Market for trading in derivatives of metals such as copper, tin, zinc etc.

London Stock Exchange (LSE)	Market for trading in securities. Formerly know as the International Stock Exchange of the United Kingdom and Republic of Ireland or ISE.
Long	A bought position in a security or derivative which is held open.
Long coupons	1) Bonds or notes with a long current maturity; 2) A coupon on which the period is longer than the others or the standard coupon period.
Long-dated	Gilts with more than 15 years until redemption.
Long position	Refers to an investor's account in which he has more shares of a specific security than he needs to meet his settlement obligations.
Lot	The common term used to describe the standard unit of trading for futures and options. It is also referred to as a "contract".
Managed fund	A unit-linked policy where the managers decide on the allocation of premiums to different unitised funds.
Mandatory event	A corporate action which affects the securities without giving any choice to the security holder.
Margin	*Initial* margin is collateral placed by one party with a counterparty or clearing house at the time of a deal, against the possibility that the market price will move against the first party, thereby leaving the counterparty with a credit risk.
Margin cont'd	*Variation* margin is a payment made, or collateral transferred, from one party to the other because the market price of the transaction or of collateral has changed. Variation margin payment is in effect either a settlement of profit/loss (e.g. in the case of a futures contract) or the reduction of credit exposure.
Margin cont'd	In a loan, margin is the extra interest above a benchmark such as LIBOR required by a lender to compensate for the credit risk of that particular borrower.
Margin cont'd	Money or assets that must be deposited by participants in securities lending, repos or OTC

derivatives markets as a guarantee that they will be able to meet their commitments at the due date.

Marginal rate of tax
The rate of tax which will apply to the next unit of income.

Mandatory quote period
Time of day during which market makers in equities are obliged to quote prices under London Stock Exchange rules.

Mark-to-market
The process of revaluing an OTC or exchange-traded product each day. It is the difference between the closing price on the previous day and the current closing price. For exchange-traded products, this is referred to as variation margin.

Market
Description of any organisation or facility through which items are traded. All exchanges are markets.

Market counterparty
A person dealing as agent or principal with the broker and involved in the same nature of investment business as the broker. This also includes fellow members of the SFA or trading members of an investment exchange, for those products only where they are members.

Market forces
Supply and demand allowing buyers and sellers to fix the price without external interference.

Market maker
A trader who works for an organisation such as an investment bank. They quote bids and offers in the market and are normally under an obligation to make a price in a certain number of contracts. They create liquidity in the contract by offering to buy or sell.

Market price
In the case of a security, the market price is usually considered as the last reported price at which the stock or bond has been sold.

Market risk
Also position risk. The risk that the market value of a position falls.

Market value
The price at which a security is trading and could presumably be purchased or sold.

Master agreement
This agreement is for OTC transactions and is signed between the client and the broker. It covers the basic terms under which the client and the

broker wish to transact business. Each individual trade has a separate individual agreement with specific terms known as a confirm.

Matching (comparison)
Another term for comparison (or checking); a matching system to compare trades and ensure that both sides of trade correspond.

Maturity
The date on which the principal or nominal value of a bond becomes due and payable in full to the holder.

Medium dated
Gilts due to be redeemed within the next 7 to 15 years.

Merchant banks
Often relatively small but prestigious financial institutions, who deal mainly with companies and wealthy individuals in providing a range of financial services including, amongst others, corporate finance and portfolio management.

Mergers and acquisition (M&A)
Divisions of securities houses or merchant banks responsible for advising on takeover activity. Usually work with the corporate finance department and is often kept as a single unit.

Mezzanine debt
A debt issue that ranks higher than equity and junior debt but lower than senior.

MiFID
Markets in Financial Instruments Directive, an European Union Directive.

Mixed economy
Economy which relies on a mix of market forces and government involvement.

Model risk
The risk that the computer model used by a bank for valuation or risk assessment is incorrect or misinterpreted.

Modified following
The convention that if a settlement date in the future falls on a non-business day, the settlement date will be moved to the next following business day. If it moves to next month, then the settlement date is moved back to the last previous business day.

Monetary interest rate
The actual interest rate received in money terms.

Money laundering
The process where criminals attempt to conceal the true origin and ownership of the proceeds of

their criminal activities and to legitimise these proceeds by introducing them into the mainstream of financial activities.

Money market The market for the purchase and sale of short-term financial instruments. Short term is usually defined as less than one year.

Money market fund An open-end mutual fund that invests in commercial paper, banker's acceptances, repurchase agreements, government securities and other highly liquid and safe securities. The fund pays money market rates of interest. Many money market funds are part of fund families; investors can switch their money from one fund to another and back again without charge.

Money rate of return Annual return as a percentage of asset value.

Money supply Measure of the money available in the economy.

M0 & M4 UK measure of the money supply that measures notes and coins (M0 or M0 Plus) and bank and building society deposits (M4).

Moody's investment Service Located in New York City with its parent, Dun & Bradstreet, Moody's is one of the two most popular bond rating agencies in the US. The other agency is Standard and Poor's.

Mortgage A form of security on borrowing commonly associated with home borrowing.

Mortgage-backed security Security backed by an investment company that raises money from shareholders and invests it in stocks, bonds or other instruments (unit trust, investment fund, SICAV – BEVEK).

Multilateral netting Trade between several counterparties in the same security are netted such that each counterparty makes only one transfer of cash or securities to another party or to a central clearing system. Handles only transactions due for settlement on the same day.

Mutual collateralisation The deposit of collateral by both counterparties to a transaction.

Mutual fund 1   A term used to describe an open-ended invest-
                      ment company or trust in the US and elsewhere,
                      same as OEIC in the UK.

Mutual fund 2   Fund operated by an investment company that
                      raises money from shareholders and invests it in
                      stocks, bonds or other instruments (unit trusts,
                      investment companies like OEICS, SICAVs are all
                      examples).

Naked option   An option bought or sold for speculation, with no
                      offsetting existing position behind it.

Naked writing   Where the seller does not own the stock corre-
                      sponding to the call option which he has sold, and
                      would be forced to pay the prevailing market price
                      for the stock to meet delivery obligations, if called.

NASDAQ   National Association of Securities Dealers Auto-
                      mated Quotation system.

**National   Trade association of pension funds through which
Association of   they can voice their opinions collectively.
Pension Funds
(NAPF)**

**National   Tax levied on income. The level of which depends
insurance**   on the amount earned subject to a ceiling and
                      payable in the UK by employer and employee.

National savings Department of government responsible for
                      running a variety of short-term borrowings. Its
                      operations are undertaken through post offices.

Negative equity   The amount by which a home purchase loan
                      exceeds the value of the property which is the
                      security for the loan.

**Net asset value   In mutual funds, the market value of the fund
(NAV)**   share. It is common practice for an investment
                      trust to compute its assets daily, or even twice a
                      day, by totalling the closing market value of all
                      securities and assets (i.e. cash) owned. All liabil-
                      ities are deducted, and the balance is divided by
                      the number of share outstanding. The resulting
                      figure is the net asset value per share.

**Net present   Also NPV. The net total of several present values
value**   (arising from cashflows at different future dates)
                      added together, some of which may be positive
                      and some negative.

Netting	Trading partners offset their positions thereby reducing the number of positions for settlement. Netting can be either *bilateral, multilateral* or *continuous net settlement.*
New issues	Company-raised additional capital by issuing new securities. New issue is the name given to the bonds or stocks offered to investors for the first time.
Nikkei Dow index	Main share index in Japan.
Nil paid rights price	Ex-rights price less the subscription price.
No-par value (NPV)	Stock with no cash value assigned on the issuance of certificates.
Nominal amount	Value stated on the face of a security (principal value, par value). Securities processing: number of securities to deliver/receive.
Nominal value of a bond	The value at which the capital, or principal, of a bond will be redeemed by the issuer. Also called par value.
Nominal value of a share	The minimum price at which a share can be issued. Also called par value.
Nominated advisor	Firm appointed to advise AIM company directors on their responsibilities. Role can be combined with that of nominated broker.
Nominate broker	Firm appointed to assist dealing in AIM securities.
Nominee	An organisation that acts as the named owner of securities on behalf of a different beneficial owner who remains anonymous to the company.
Non-callable	Cannot be redeemed by the issuer for a stated period of time from date of issue.
Non-clearing member	A member of an exchange who does not undertake to settle their derivatives business. This type of member must appoint a clearing member to register all their trades at the clearing organisation.
Non-competitive bid	Bidding for a specific amount of securities without mentioning a price in an auction. Usually, the price paid will be equal to the average of the accepted competitive bids.

Non-cumulative preference share	If the company fails to pay a preference dividend, the entitlement to the dividend is simply lost. There is no accumulation.
Non-deliverable forward	A foreign exchange forward outright where, instead of each party delivering the full amount of currency at settlement, there is a single net cash payment to reflect the change in value between the forward rates transacted and the spot rate two working days before settlement.
Non-private customer	A person who is not a private customer or who has requested to be treated as a non-private customer.
Non-profit policy	An endowment or whole life policy where the benefit is a guaranteed sum only.
Non-voting shares	Some companies have two types of shares. In such cases, voting shares are restricted to owners and directors to maintain control, whereas non-voting shares are generally priced lower offsetting normal shareholders rights.
Normal bonus	The annual bonus paid on a with-profits policy.
Normal market size (NMS)	Minimum size in which market makers must quote on LSE.
Nostro	A bank's nostro account is its currency account held with a foreign bank.
Nostro reconciliation	Checking the entries shown on the bank's nostro account statement with the bank's internal records (the accounting ledgers) to ensure that they correspond exactly.
Note	Bonds issued with a relatively short maturity are often called notes.
Notional	Contracts for differences require a notional principal amount on which settlement can be calculated.
Novation	The process where registered trades are cancelled with the clearing members and substituted by two new ones – one between the clearing house and the clearing member seller, the other between the clearing house and the clearing member buyer.
NSCC	National Securities Clearing Corporation – clearing organisation for US shares.

OASYS Trade confirmation system for brokers operated by Thomson Financial Services.

OATs Obligations Assimilables du Tresor – a 7–10-year French Treasury bond.

Obligation netting An arrangement to transfer only the net amount (of cash or a security) due between two or more parties, rather than transfer all amounts between the parties on a gross basis.

Occupational pension scheme A pension scheme set up by an employer for the benefit of the employees.

Off-balance sheet A transaction whose principal amount is not shown on the balance sheet because it is a contingent liability or settled as a contract for differences.

Offer for sale Historically, the most popular form of new issue in the UK for companies bringing their securities to the stock-market for the first time. The company offers its shares to the general public.

Offer price The price at which a trader or market maker is willing to sell a contract.

Office of fair trading (OFT) Government department which advises the Secretary of State for Trade and Industry on whether or not a proposed takeover should be referred to the MMC for full investigation.

Offshore Relates to locations outside the controls of domestic monetary, exchange and legislative authorities. Offshore may not necessarily be outside the national boundaries of a country. In some countries, certain banks or other institutions may be granted offshore status and thus beexempt from all or specific controls or legislation, for example Dublin, Luxembourg.

Offshore financial centre Another name for an international financial centre.

Omnibus account Account containing the holdings of more than one client.

On-balance sheet A transaction whose principal amount is shown on the balance sheet.

Online Processing which is executed via an interactive input onto a PC or stationary terminal connected to a processing centre.

Open economy   A country where there are no restrictions on trading with other countries.

Open-ended   Type of investment such as Unit Trusts or OEICs which can expand without limit.

Open-ended investment company (OEIC)   New corporate structure introduced in 1997. It is a form of collective investment vehicle.

Open order   A purchase or sale order at a stated price that is good until cancelled or executed.

Open outcry   The style of trading whereby traders face each other in a designated area such as a pit and shout or call their respective bids and offers. Hand signals are also used to communicate. It is governed by exchange rules.

Opening trade   A bought or sold trade that is held open to create a position.

Open interest   The number of contracts both bought and sold which remain open for delivery on an exchange. Important indicator for liquidity.

Open position   The number of contracts which have not been off-set at the clearing organisation by the close of business.

Operational risk   The risk of losses resulting from inadequate systems and control, human errors or management failings.

Option   An option is – in the case of the **buyer** – the right, but not the obligation, to take (call) or make (put) for delivery of the underlying product; and – in the case of the **seller** – the obligation to make or take delivery of the underlying product.

Option premium   The sum of money paid by the buyer, for acquiring the right of the option. It is the sum of money received by the seller for incurring the obligation, having sold the rights, of the option. It is the sum of the intrinsic value and the time value.

Optional dividend   Dividend that can be paid either in cash or in stock. The shareholders entitled to the dividend make the choice.

Options on futures
These have the same characteristics as an option, the difference being that the underlying product is either a long or short futures contract. Premium is not exchanged as the contracts are marked to market each day.

Order driven market
A stock market where brokers acting on behalf of clients match trades with each other either on the trading floor of the exchange or through a central computer system.

Ordinary shares
Known as common stock in the US and equities in the UK. Shareholders are the owners of a company and are protected so the maximum loss is the value of their shares and not the full debt of the company. Ordinary shares are divided into preferred and deferred ordinaries.

Oversubscribed
Circumstances where people have applied for more shares than are available in a new issue.

Out-of-the-money
A call option whose exercise price is above the current underlying share price, or a put option whose exercise price is below the current underlying share price. This option has no intrinsic value.

Out-of-pocket expenses
Market charges which are charged to the client without taking any profit.

Out-trade
A trade which has been incorrectly matched on the floor of an exchange.

Over-the-counter (OTC)
A one-to-one agreement between two counterparties where the specifications of the product are completely flexible and non-standardised.

Overdraft
Withdrawal of more money than is in a bank account at a given time.

Overnight money
Money placed on the money market for repayment for the next day.

Oversold
Where a rush of selling shares has depressed the market for no justifiable reason. Can also be a term used to describe a dealing error, that is sold 100 instead of 10.

Own life policy
Life assurance policy taken out on the life of the policy holder.

Panel on takeovers and mergers (PTM)	A non-statutory body comprising City institutions, which regulates takeover activities.
Par value	See *nominal value* of a bond/share.
Pair off	Back-to-back trade between two parties where settlement occurs only by exchanging the cash difference between the two parties.
Pari passu	Without partiality. Securities that rank pari passu rank equally with each other.
Paying agent	A bank which handles payment of interest and dividends on behalf of the issuer of a security.
Payment date	Date on which a dividend or an interest payment is scheduled to be paid.
P/E Ratio	The ratio of share price to earnings in assessing the rating of a company. The ratio is calculated by taking the net profit of the company and dividing it by the number of shares on issue. This gives the earnings per share. The P/E ratio is arrived at by dividing this figure into the share price.
Pension fund	Fund set up by a corporation, labour union, governmental entity or other organisation to pay the pension benefits of retired workers. Pension funds invest billions of dollars annually in the securities markets and are therefore major market players.
Perpetual bond	A bond which has no redemption date.
Person assured	The person taking out a life assurance policy. Not necessarily the same as the life assured.
Personal equity plan (PEP)	Investment scheme whereby investors buy shares through a PEP manager; all profits and dividends being tax free (cannot be taken out anymore).
Personal pension scheme	A pension scheme entered into with an insurance company (or other provider) individually by an employee or a self employed person.
PIK	A payment in kind, i.e. shares in lieu of a cash payment.
PIPE	Private investment in a public entity. A PIPE is a possible alternative available to publicly

traded companies that need to raise money, often relatively small amounts, but do not want to go through the complexity of going through a secondary offering like a rights issue. Instead, the company finds an investor and sells him a block of newly issued shares at an agreed price or a block of debt which can later be converted into shares (a structured PIPE).

Placement   The first stage of money laundering in which the money is passed or placed in the banking system. See layering, integration.

Placing   Procedure used for new issues where a securities house contracts its own clients to offer them stock. It is almost always used for new issues of eurobonds and for equities on the London Stock Exchange more so since January 1996 when restrictions on their use were removed.

Plain vanilla or   A swap which has a very basic structure.
vanilla swap

Poison Pill   Strategic move by a company that is the target of a takeover to make its stock less attractive to an acquirer. As a defence, the company can issue Poison Pill Rights.

Poison Pill   This is an anti-takeover defence used by corpo-
Rights   rations. A company will approve a Rights plan. The Rights are usually "associated" with the firm's common stock and will only be physically issued and exercisable following designated events, i.e. hostile suitor acquires 10% of the company's stock etc. The Rights allow current holders to purchase additional shares at a bargain price, thus raising the cost of an acquisition and causing dilution. To counter this, hostile tender offers are usually conditioned upon the Rights being redeemed or otherwise made void.

Portfolio   List of investments held by an individual or company, or list of loans made by a bank or financial institution.

Power of   The legal authority for one party to sign for and
attorney   act on behalf of another party.

Pre-emption rights

The right of existing shareholders purchase shares in a new issue to maintain their percentage holding. Normally happens either when a company is trying to raise cash or as a result of a takeover for paper which the seller does not want.

Preference shares

Shares that have preferential rights to dividends, usually a fixed sum, before dividends are paid out to ordinary shareholders. They usually carry no voting rights. The rights of preference shareholders are established in a company's articles of association and may differ between companies in a variety of ways.

Premium

An option premium is the amount paid upfront by the purchaser of the option to the writer.

Present value

The amount of money which needs to be invested (or borrowed) now at a given interest rate in order to achieve exactly a given cash-flow in the future, assuming compound re-investment (or re-funding) of any interest payments received (or paid) before the end. See future value.

Pre-settlement

Checks and procedures undertaken immediately after execution of a trade prior to settlement.

Price/earnings ratio

The share price of a company divided by its earnings per share. A high price/earnings ratio implies that the company is well thought of for its future prospects. See also P/E Ratio.

Price (conversion) factor

The price at which a bond would trade, per one nominal, to yield the notional coupon of the futures contract on the delivery day (or the first day in the deliverable month if this applies).

Primary dealer

See *gilt-edged market maker.*

Primary market

Market for the placement of new securities such as international, domestic and foreign bond issues. Any subsequent resale or purchase is handled on the secondary market.

Prime broker Broker providing a wide range of services including execution, stock lending, loans, sales etc. to funds, particularly hedge funds.

Prime rate Term used in US banks for the rate at which they lend to prime or first class customers. Similar to the base rate in the UK.

Principal-protected product An investment whose maturity value is guaranteed to be at least the principal amount invested initially.

Principal trading When a member firm of the London Stock Exchange buys stock from or sells stock to a non-member.

Principal-to-principal market A market where the clearing house only recognises the clearing member as one entity, and not the underlying clients of the clearing member.

Principal value That amount inscribed on the face of a security and exclusive of interest or premium. The amount is the one used in the computation of interest due on sucha security.

Private customer An individual person who is not acting in the course of carrying on investment business.

Private equity Shares in an unlisted company.

Private placement Issue of securities that is offered to a limited number of investor.

Privatisation Process whereby the government puts state-owned industries into the private sector, e.g. water, electricity. Usually involves an offer for sale of its shares.

Proprietary trader A trader who deals for an organisation such as an investment bank taking advantage of short-term price movements as well as taking long-term views on whether the market will move up or down.

Prospectus See *listing particulars*.

Proxy Appointee of a shareholder who votes on his behalf at company meetings.

Proxy statement Material information to be given to a corporation's stockholders prior to solicitation of votes.

Public sector net cash requirement (PSNCR)
Shortfall of government revenue over expenditure, which it needs to borrow. (This shortfall was until June 1998 known as the public sector borrowing requirement – PSBR.)

Public offering
Offer of securities to the general public.

Public placement
An issue of securities that is offered through a securities house to institutional and individual clients.

Put option
An option that gives the buyer the right, but not the obligation, to sell a specified quantity of the underlying asset at a fixed price, on or before a specified date. The seller of a put option has the obligation (because they have sold the right) to take delivery of the underlying asset if the option is exercised by the buyer.

Quoted
Colloquial term for a security that is traded on the stock exchange.

Quote driven
Dealing system where some firms accept the responsibility to quote buying and selling prices.

Ramp
A method employed to inflate a share price with the intention of selling before the price drops back again.

Range forward
A forward outright with two forward rates, where settlement takes place at the higher forward rate if the spot rate at maturity is higher than that, at the lower forward rate if the spot rate at maturity is lower than that or at the spot rate at maturity otherwise. See collar.

Rating
Evaluation of securities investment and credit risk by rating services such as Moody's or Standard and Poor's.

RCH
Recognised Clearing House under the Financial Services Act.

Real interest rate
The rate of interest after taking inflation into account.

Real time gross settlement
Gross settlement system where trades are settled continuously through the processing day – abbreviated to RTGS.

Realised profit Profit which has arisen from a real sale.

Receiver Person, usually an accountant, appointed by creditors in an attempt to rescue an ailing company through tighter financial controls than were already in place. Generally, they succeed only in utilizing the company assets to reimburse secured creditors after which any remaining creditors can appoint a liquidator.

Recession Temporary reduction in trade that affects a downturn in the economy. A number of causes can create this situation such as falling share and property prices, lack of consumer confidence, unemployment etc.

Recognised investment exchange (RIE) Status given by a regulatory body to an approved exchange.

Reconciliation The comparison of a person's records of cash and securities position with records held by another party and the investigation and resolution of any discrepancies between the two sets of records.

Record date The date on which a securities holder must hold the securities in order to receive an income or entitlement.

Redemption The purchase and cancellation of outstanding securities through a cash payment to the holder.

Redemption price A price at which bonds may be redeemed, or called, at the issuer's option, prior to maturity (often with a slight premium).

Referral If a proposed takeover is investigated thoroughly by the MMC, the procedure is that it is referred to the MMC by the secretary of state for trade and industry.

Registered bond A bond whose owner is registered with the issuer or its registrar.

Registered title Form of ownership of securities where the owner's name appears on a register maintained by the company.

Registrar An official of a company who maintains its share register.

Registrar of companies Government department responsible for keeping records of all companies.

Reinsurance

The sharing of risk amongst insurance companies where the liability would be too great for one to take on alone. For example, an oil refinery may have an insured risk to the value of £300–400 million. Up to 20 insurance companies may have a percentage liability for that risk.

Reorganisation

Generally, any event where the equity, debt or capital structure of a company is changed.

Repayment mortgage

A mortgage loan which is repaid systematically throughout the life of the mortgage.

Replacement cost

The mark-to-market loss which would be incurred if it were necessary to undertake a new transaction to replace an existing one, because the existing counterparty defaulted.

Repurchase agreement (repo)

Borrowing funds by providing a government security for collateral and promising to 'repurchase' the security at the end of the agreed upon time period. The associated interest rate is the 'repo-rate'.

Reputational risk

The risk that an organisation's reputation will be damaged.

Reserve currency

The trading balance of a country, normally held in readily convertible currencies such as sterling, dollars, yen etc.

Reserves

The assets of a country are made up of, in part, its financial reserves such as gold, convertible currency, International Monetary Fund credits and special drawing rights. Other assets include property, overseas investments etc.

Residence

The status determining the extent to which a person is taxed in a country with a global system of taxation. Residence is determined according to periods of physical presence in the country.

Resolution

Proposal on which shareholders vote, put them at a meeting.

Retail price index (RPI)

Index that shows the movement of prices in the UK.

Reverse repo

Purchase of gilt where the price and date for its re-sale is fixed at the same time.

Reverse takeover	The acquisition of a company by a smaller concern. Can also apply where a large organisation takes over a smaller one but the overall running of the amalgamated company would be by the latter.
Reverse yield gap	Usually, equities produce a higher yield than bonds. When the converse applies it is known as the Reverse Yield Gap.
RIE	A Recognised Investment Exchange designated by a regulatory authority.
Rights issue	Offer of shares made to existing shareholders.
Right of offset	Where positions and cash held by the Clearing Organisation in different accounts for a member are allowed to be netted.
Risk warning	Document that must be despatched and signed by private customers before they deal in traded options.
Roller coaster swap	A swap in which the notional principal amount varies up and down over the life of the swap.
Roll-over	A Libor fixing on a new tranche of loan, or transfer of a futures position to the next delivery month.
Rolling settlement	System used in most countries including England. Bargains are settled a set number of days after being transacted.
Round lot	The minimum amount for which a dealer's quotes are good.
Round tripping	The combined commission or fees for both the opening and the closing legs of a trade.
Running a book	Firms who are buying and selling stock for themselves hoping to profit from price differences are said to run a book in that stock.
Safekeeping	Holding of securities on behalf of clients. They are free to sell at any time.
Sale of rights nil paid	The sale of the entitlement to take up a rights issue – see also nil paid price.
Same day funds	Refers to the availability of funds on the same day as they are deposited.
Samurai bond	A bond denominated in JPY and issued in the Japanese capital market by a foreign borrower.

Savings account   An interest bearing account with a bank or other savings institution which normally does not provide cheque and other transaction facilities.

Sawtooth risk   A swap in which the notional principal amount varies up and down over the life of the swap, with an overall upward or downward trend.

Scaling down   When a new issue is over subscribed, the procedure whereby applicants receive a proportion of the number of shares for which they applied.

Scrip dividends   Scrip dividends often provide shareholders with the choice of receiving dividend entitlements in the form of cash, share or a combination of both. The amount of stocks to be distributed under a scrip option is calculated by dividing the cash dividend amount by the average market price over a recent period of time.

Scrip issue   See *bonus issue*.

Secondary market   Marketplace for trading in existing securities. The price at which they are trading has no direct effect on the company's fortunes but is a reflection of investors' perceptions of the company.

Secured   A debt issued by a company that is charged against an asset, or a private transaction like a mortgage, where the property is charged against the loan to purchase it.

Securitisation   The use of securities and other assets to guarantee the repayment of a debt. An example would be using the rents from a property to guarantee a bond that is issued to raise capital to purchase more property.

Securities   Bonds and equities.

Securities house   General term covering any type of organisation involved in securities although usually reserved for the larger firms.

Securities lending Loan of securities by an investor to another (usually a broker-dealer), usually to cover a short sale.

Securities and Exchange Commission (SEC)   The overall investment regulatory body in the US.

SEDOL	Stock Exchange Daily Official List, a securities numbering system assigned by the International Stock Exchange in London.
Segregated account	Account in which there is only the holdings of one client.
Segregation of funds	Where the client assets are held separately from those assets belonging to the member firm.
Selective marketing	See *placing*.
Self regulating organisations (SROs)	Bodies which receive their status from FSA and are able to regulate sectors of the financial services industry. Membership of an SRO provides authorisation.
SETS	London Stock Exchange Trading System.
Settlement	The fulfilment of the contractual commitments of transacted business.
Settlement Date	The date on which a trade is cleared by delivery of securities against funds (actual settlement date, contractual settlement date).
Settlor	The person setting up a trust.
17F-5 Regulation	Legal requirements for worldwide correspondent banks which serve US mutual funds, pension funds and other regulated financial groups.
Share futures	Based on individual shares. Delivery is fulfilled by the payment or receipt of cash against the exchange-calculated delivery settlement price.
Share option	A right sold to an investor conferring the option to buy or sell shares of a particular company at a predetermined price and within a specified time limit.
Shell company	A company in name only but quoted on the stock exchange. Shells are used when setting up a new business avoiding the sometimes long and expensive process.
Shogun bond	Straight bond denominated in foreign currency, other than JPY, issued by a foreign issuer on the Japanese capital market.
Short	A sold position in a derivative which is held open.
Short coupons	Bonds or notes with a short current maturity.

Short cover   The purchase of a security that has been previously sold short. The purpose is to return securities that were borrowed to make a delivery.

Short-dated gilt   Gilts due to be redeemed within the next 7 years, according to the LSE (FT states up to 5 years).

Short position   The selling of securities, commodities etc. which are not owned.

Short sale   The sale of securities not owned by the seller in the expectation that the price of these securities will fall or as part of an arbitrage.

Short selling   Selling stock that you do not own.

Short-term security Generally, an obligation maturing in less than one year. A very short investment horizon.

Short termism   Fund managers expect prices of shares in which they have invested to rise quickly and are not willing to exert influence on management to improve corporate performance but prefer to sell the shares.

Simple interest   Interest calculated on the assumption that there is no opportunity to re-invest the interest payments during the life of an investment and thereby earn extra income.

Single currency Interest rate swap An interest rate swap where the interest payments are exchanged in the same currency.

Sinking fund   In the case of a loan repaid by instalments, each instalment can be considered to consist of two parts. One portion of each instalment represents the interest payable on the loan, the other portion, which represents the repayment of capital, is known as the "sinking fund".

Slump   An excessive long-term recession with disastrous economic implications.

Soft commodities   Description given to commodities such as sugar, coffee and cocoa, traded through LIFFE since its incorporation of the former London Commodity Exchange (LCE).

Sovereign debt securities Bonds issued by the government of a country.

SPAN   Standardised Portfolio Analysis of Risk. A form of margin calculation which is used by various clearing organisations.

Speculation   A deal undertaken because the dealer expects prices to move in his favour and thereby realise a profit.

Speculator   The speculator is a trader who wants to assume risk for potentially much higher rewards.

Sponsored member Type of CREST member whose name appears on the register but has no computer link with CREST.

Spot delivery A delivery or settlement of currencies on the value date, two business days later.

Spot market   Market for immediate as opposed to future delivery. In the spot market for foreign exchange, settlement is in two business days ahead.

Spot month   The first month for which futures contracts are available.

Spot rate   The price prevailing in the spot market.

Spread
1) The difference between bid and asked price on a security
2) Difference between yield on or prices of two securities of different types or maturities
3) In underwriting, difference between price realised by an issuer and price paid by the investor
4) Difference between two prices or two rates. What commodities traders would refer to as the basis.

Spread cont'd A trading strategy in which a trader buys one instrument and sells another, related instrument with a view to profiting from a change in the price difference between the two. A futures spread is the purchase of one futures contract and the sale of another; an option spread is the purchase of one call (or put) and the sale of another.

Spread cont'd The difference between the bid and offer prices in a quotation.

Spread cont'd The difference between one price or rate and another, e.g. the extent to which a swap fixed-rate is higher than a benchmark Treasury bond yield, or the extent to which the floating rate in a swap is above or below LIBOR.

SPV   Short for special purpose vehicle, a company, fund etc. established for a specific reason such as a private equity fund etc.

Stag   Someone who applies for a new issue of shares intending to sell them (at a profit) as soon as secondary market dealings start.

Stamp duty   Tax on purchase of equities in the UK.

Stamp duty reserve tax (SDRT) (UK)   Tax payable on the purchase of UK equities in uncertified form (i.e. those held within CREST).

Standard settlement instructions   Instructions for settlement with a particular counterparty which are always followed for a particular kind of deal and, once in place, are therefore not repeated at the time of each transaction.

Standing instruction   Default instruction, e.g. provided to an agent processing payments or clearing securities trades; provided by shareholder on how to vote shares (e.g. vote for all management recommended candidates).

Standing order   An instruction to a bank to pay regular agreed amounts on specified dates. These cannot be altered by the bank.

Stepped   A stepped coupon is one that rises or falls in a predetermined way over the life of an arrangement.

Stock   In some countries (e.g. US), the term applies to ordinary share capital of a company. In other countries (e.g. UK), stock may mean share capital that is issued in variable amount instead of in fixed specified amounts, or it can describe government loans.

Stock dividend   Dividends paid by a company in stock instead of cash.

Stock exchange electronic trading system (SETS)   Electronic dealing system for some stocks on the London Stock Exchange.

Stockmarket
Term used to describe where securities are/have been traded, i.e. "today on the stockmarket shares closed higher".

Stock index futures/options
Based on the value of an underlying stock index like the FTSE 100 in the UK, the S & P 500 index in the US and the Nikkei 225 and 300 in Japan. Delivery is fulfilled by the payment or receipt of cash against the exchange-calculated delivery settlement price. These are referred to as indices or indexes.

Stock (or bond) power
A legal document, either on the back of registered stocks and bonds or attached to them, by which the owner assigns his interest in the corporation to a third party, allowing that party the right to substitute another name on the company records instead of the original owner's.

Stock split
When a corporation splits its stock, it divides.

Stop (order)
An owner of a physical security that has been mutilated, lost or stolen will request the issuer to place a stop (transfer) on the security and to cancel and replace the security.

Straight debt
A standard bond issue, without right to convert into the common shares of the issuer.

Straddle
The purchase of a call combined with the purchase of a put at the same strike (generally purchased with both at-the-money).

Straight-through processing
Computer transmission of the details of a trade, without manual intervention, from their original input by the trader to all other relevant areas – position keeping, risk control, accounts, settlement, reconciliation.

Street name
Securities held in street name are held in the name of a broker or another nominee, i.e. a customer.

Strike price
The fixed price, per share or unit, at which an option conveys the right to call (purchase) or put (sell) the underlying shares or units.

Strike price/rate
Also exercise price. The price or rate at which the holder of an option can insist on the underlying transaction being fulfilled.

Strip   The purchase or sale of a series of consecutive interest rate futures contracts or forward rate agreements.

Stripped bonds (strips)   Bonds where the rights to the interest payments and eventual repayment of the nominal value have been separated from each other and traded independently. Facility introduced for gilts in December 1997.

Stump period   A calculation period, usually at the beginning or end of a swap, other than the standard ones normally quoted.

Subcustodian   A bank in a foreign country that acts on behalf of the custodian as its custody agent.

Subscription price   Price at which shareholders of a corporation are entitled to purchase shares in a rights offering or at which subscription warrants are exercisable. Amount to be paid on the offering of shares or units in a new fund.

Subscriptions   The buying orders from the lead manager, co-managers, underwriters and selling group members for the securities being offered.

Subsidiary   A company at least 50% of which is owned by another company. See *holding company*.

Surrender value   The value for which a life assurance policy can be cashed in for prior to maturity.

Swap   Arrangement where two borrowers, one of whom has fixed interest and one of whom has floating rate borrowings, swap their commitments with each other. A bank would arrange the swap and charge a fee.

SwapClear   A clearing house and central counterparty for swaps.

SwapsWire   An electronic dealing system for swaps.

Swaption   An option into a predetermined swap transaction. Options can be payers or receivers, American or European.

SWIFT   Society for Worldwide Interbank Financial Telecommunications – secure electronic communications network between banks.

Switching The facility to move the money invested in a unit linked policy from one fund to another.

Syndicate A group of bond houses which act together in underwriting and distributing a new securities issue.

Tactical asset allocation The temporary changing of the composition of the portfolio to take advantage of short-term market opportunities and fluctuations.

Takeover When one company obtains more than 50% of another company's shares.

Tap stocks A portion of gilt-edged securities that are held over after the day of issue and made available by the government broker to satisfy demand and to control interest rates, market prices and liquidity.

TARGET Trans European Automated Real time Gross settlement Express Transfer – system linking the real-time gross settlements for euros in the European Union countries.

Tax avoidance The legitimate arrangement of a taxpayer's affairs so that he receives income or gains in such a way that it takes him out of the tax regime altogether or reduces his tax liability. Tax avoidance is not illegal.

Tax evasion Tax evasion means ignoring or concealing a tax liability which has already arisen. Tax evasion is a criminal offence.

Tax exempt special savings account (TESSA) Scheme whereby certain savings plans will generate interest, free of income tax (now unavailable).

Tax haven Another name for an international financial centre where favourable tax laws apply.

Tax reclaim The process that a global custodian and/or a holder of securities performs, in accordance with local government filing requirements, in order to recapture a allowable percentage of taxed withheld.

TechMark Market on the LSE for technology-related stocks.

Telephone banking Convenience banking set up to avoid restrictions and delays experienced at traditional branches.

Tender offer   Formal offer to buy made to holders of a particular issue by a third party. Detailed offer is made by public announcement in newspapers and sometimes by personal letter of transmittal to each stockholder.

Terms   For a new securities issue, the characteristics of the securities on offer: coupon, amount, maturity.

Term assurance   The sum assured becomes payable if the life assured dies during a specified period of time. There is no savings element.

Terminal bonus   A bonus paid on the maturity of a with-profits policy.

Termination date   The end date of a swap.

Territorial system of tax   A tax system whereby a country levies tax only on an income arising in the country and not on overseas income.

Thin market   A period of sparse trade on the stock market that can affect prices and the ability to trade.

Thomson report   An electronic transaction reporting system for international equities on the London Stock Exchange operated by Thomson.

Tick size   The value of a one point movement in the contract price.

Tied agent   An individual or business which only sells one company's products (such as life assurance) making no pretext of offering independent advice on all the products available.

Time deposit   Deposit on an account held with a financial institution for a fixed term or with the understanding that the depositor can withdraw only by giving notice.

Time value   The amount by which an option's premium exceeds its intrinsic value. Where an option has no intrinsic value the premium consists entirely of time value.

Tom-Next   Money placed on the money market from tomorrow for repayment the day after.

Tom/spot week   Money placed on the money market from tomorrow for repayment one week after (Tom/Spot Month).

Touch
The best prices available for a stock on the stock-market, looking at all market makers.

Tracker fund
See *index funds*.

Trade date
The date on which a trade is made.

Trade guarantees
Guarantees in place in a market which ensure that all compared or netted trades will be settled as compared regardless of a counterparty default.

Traded option
An option which is traded on an exchange.

Trader
An individual who buys and sells securities with the objective of making short-term gains.

Trading permits
These are issued by exchanges and give the holder the right to have one trader at any one time trading in the contract(s) to which the permit relates.

Transfer
Change of ownership of securities.

Transfer agent
Agent appointed by a fund to maintain records (register) of share or unit owners, to cancel and issue certificates and to resolve problems arising from lost, destroyed or stolen certificates.

Transfer form
Document which owners of registered documents must sign when they sell the security. Not required where a book entry transfer system is in use.

Transparency
The degree to which a market is characterised by prompt availability of accurate price and volume information which gives participants full knowledge of the details of transactions being executed on the exchange.

TRAX
Trade confirmation system for the euro-markets operated by ISMA.

Treasury
Arm of government responsible for all financial decisions and regulation of the financial services sector.

Treasury bill
Money market instrument issued with a life of less than one year by the US and UK governments.

Treasury bonds (US)
US government bond issued with a 30 year maturity.

Treasury note
A government obligation with maturities of 1 to 10 years, carrying a fixed rate of interest.

Treasury notes (US)	US government bond issued with 2, 3, 5 and 7 year maturity.
Tri-party repo	Repo which utilises an intermediary custodian to oversee the exchange of securities and cash.
Triple A – rating (AAA)	The highest credit rating for a bond or company – the risk of default (or non-payment) is negligible.
Trust	A legal arrangement where one person (the trustee) holds property (the trust property) on behalf of one or more other persons (the beneficiaries).
Trust property	The property put into trust by the settlor.
Trustee	Trustees are appointed to oversee the management of certain funds. They are responsible for ensuring that the fund is managed correctly and that the interest of the investor are protected and that all relevant regulations and legislation are complied with.
Turn	See *spread*.
Turnaround	Securities bought and sold for settlement on the same day.
Turnaround time	The time available or needed to settle a turnaround trade.
Two-way price	Simultaneous prices in a stock quoted by a market maker, the lower at which he is willing to buy and the higher at which he is willing to sell.
UCITS	Undertakings for Collective Investments in Transferable Securities, a European Union Directive
Uncovered dividends	A dividend that is not paid out of profits and therefore means that the organisation has had to liquidate assets to make the payments.
Underlying asset	The asset from which the future or option's price is derived.
Undersubscribed	Circumstance when people have applied for fewer shares than are available in a new issue.
Underwrite	Accept financial responsibility for (a commercial project); sign and issue (an insurance policy), thus accepting liability.
Underwriter	As part of a syndicate, a dealer who purchases new issues from the issuer and distributes them to investors.

Underwriters	Institutions which agree to take up shares in a new issue if it is undersubscribed. They will charge an underwriting fee.
Unit investment trust	A close end fund used by small investors to spread investment risk.
Unit-linked policy	An endowment or whole life policy which invests in a unitised fund and the value of the policy is the value of the units purchased.
Unit trust	A fund whereby money from a number of investors is pooled together and invested collectively on their behalf. Each owns a unit (or number of them) the value of which depends on the value of those items owned by the trust. Established under trust law not company law.
Unrealised profit	Profit that has not arisen from a sale – an increase in value of an asset.
Up-and-in option	A knock-in option where the trigger is higher than the underlying rate at the start. See down-and-in option, up-and-out option, down-and-out option.
Up-and-out option	A knock-out option where the trigger is higher than the underlying rate at the start. See up-and-in option, down-and-in option, down-and-out option.
Value added tax	A type of sales tax.
Value at risk (VaR)	The maximum amount which a bank expects to lose, with a given confidence level, over a given time period.
Variation margin	The process of revaluing an exchange-traded product each day. It is the difference between the closing price on the previous day against the current closing price. It is physically paid or received each day by the clearing organisation. It is often referred to as the mark-to-market.
Venture capital	Funds that are utilized to back or buy-out unquoted companies.
Venture capital trusts	Trusts set up to encourage investment in small- and medium-sized businesses by investing in a range of companies thereby reducing some of the risk.

Vestima   Service offered by Clearstream for settlement etc. of investment funds.

Volatility   The degree of scatter of the underlying price when compared to the mean average rate.

Vostro   A vostro account is another bank's account held at our bank in our currency.

Wall Street   Term used to describe the financial centre around the New York Stock Exchange, which is situated on the corner of Wall Street. Much the same as the Square Mile in London is known as the City.

Warrants   An option which can be listed on an exchange, with a lifetime of generally more than one year.

Warrant agent   A bank appointed by the issuer as an intermediary between the issuing company and the (physical) warrant holders, interacting when the latter want to exercise the warrants.

Wealth tax   A tax charged on the wealth of an individual during their lifetime.

Weekly Official Intelligence (WOI)   Weekly publication by the London Stock Exchange which provides (amongst other things) a summary of company announcements during that week.

White knight   A preferred bidder in the case of a takeover where it is considered that the alternatives may be detrimental, e.g. management changes and/or the dismemberment of the company.

Whole life insurance   The benefits of the policy become payable on the death of the life assured.

With-profits policy   An endowment or whole life policy which participates in the investment performance of the life company through the allocation of normal and terminal bonuses.

Withholding tax   In the securities industry, a tax imposed by a government's tax authorities on dividends and interest paid.

World Bank   Survivor along with the International Monetary Fund of the 1944 Bretton Woods agreement. Officially the International Bank for

	Reconstruction and Development, its aim is to lend or guarantee loans to poorer countries by utilizing aid from member countries.
Writer	A person who has sold an open derivatives contract and is obliged to deliver or take delivery upon notification of exercise from the buyer.
Yankee bond	A US dollar bond issued in the US by a non-US issuer.
Yield	Internal rate of return expressed as a percentage.
Yield curve	For securities that expose the investor to the same credit risk, a graph showing the relationship at a given point in the time between yield and current maturity. Yield curves are typically drawn using yields on governments of various maturities.
Yield to maturity	The rate of return yielded by a debt security held to maturity when both interest payments and the investor's capital gain or loss on the security are taken into account.
Zero coupon bond	A bond issued with no coupon but a price substantially below par so that only capital is accrued over the life of the loan, and yield is comparable to coupon bearing instruments.

Useful websites and suggested further reading

Websites

www.aima.org	Alternative Investment Management Association
www.bis.org	Bank for International Settlement
www.clearstream.com	Clearstream
www.clsbank.com	CLS Bank
www.dscportfolio.com	The Derivatives and Securities Consultancy Ltd
www.euroclear.com	Euroclear
www.euronext.com	Euronext
www.fsa.gov.uk	Financial Services Authority
www.fundadmin.com	
www.ici.org	Investment Company Institute
www.indiavca.org	Indian Venture Capital Association
www.investopedia.com	Investopedia
www.isda.com	International Swaps and Derivatives Association
www.isma.co.uk	International Securities Markets Association
www.issanet.org	International Securities Services Association
www.jerseyfinance.je	Jersey Finance Online

www.londonstockexchange.com   The London Stock Exchange
www.sec.gov   Securities and Exchange
                               Commission
www.sii.org.uk   The Securities and Investment
                               Institute

Suggested further reading

- Understanding the Financial Markets*
- Managing Technology in the Operations Function*
- Clearing, Settlement and Custody*
- Controls Procedures and Risk*
- Clearing and Settlement of Derivatives*
- Operations Risk*

   Published by Elsevier.

- Mastering Treasury Operations
- Understanding Foreign Exchange and Currency Options

   Published by FT Prentice Hall.

- Global Operations Management*
- Advanced Global Operations Management*

   Published by Wiley.

visUlearn™ series of CD ROMs*

- Equities & Bonds
- Derivatives & Commodities
- Operations – Clearing, Settlement & Custody
- An Overview of the Financial Services Industry

Periodicals

- Funds Europe – *published by Funds Europe Ltd*
- Portfolio International – *published by Newsquest Specialist Media Ltd www.portfolio-international.com*

---

* Order from www.dscporfolio.com or call 0207 403 8383 quoting websites/reading for a major discount.

Appendix 1

OEICS or retail funds/trusts and hedge funds differ in many ways. The main areas of difference that can be highlighted are

- Type of investor
- Fees and charges including performance fees
- Investment strategies and products used
- Level of risk
- Pricing
- Ability to sell shares/units (liquidity)
- Regulatory oversight.

For instance in most jurisdictions retail funds are among the most strictly regulated financial products. As such they are subject to numerous requirements designed to ensure that they are operated in the best interests of their investors. By comparison hedge funds are private funds, still pooled investments but subject to far less regulatory oversight.

However this is changing and for instance in the United States the SEC adopted in 2004 new rules requiring hedge fund advisers to register with the SEC under the Investment Advisers Act of 1940.

Regulatory differences

Retail funds

Investment companies, mutual funds and unit trusts are obliged to register with the local regulator such as the Financial Services Authority (FSA) in the UK or the Securities and Exchange Commission (SEC) in the US.

This means that these funds are authorized for sale to the investing public as well as others and as such are subject to rigorous regulatory oversight. Virtually every aspect of an authorized unit trust or fund's structure and operation is subject to strict regulation under various laws. Examples of these would be the FSMA in the UK and the Securities Act of 1933, the Securities Exchange Act of 1934, the Investment Company Act of 1940 and the Investment Advisers Act in the US.

The regulation relates, amongst others, to areas such as:

- Diversification of investment (minimum number of different products from different issuers thereby reducing the risk of a fund losing all its value)
- Structure and responsibilities of Directors (owners/sponsors), managers, administrators, trustees (in the US 75 per cent of a fund's directors and the fund Chairman must be independent from the investment management)*
- Marketing and sales
- Distribution of income
- Publishing of the net asset value
- Communication with investors
- Purchase and sale procedures for shares/units in the fund.

* *Source:* Investment Company Institute.

Hedge funds

As noted above hedge funds are private pooled investments subject to the terms of an investment agreement or similar document entered into by the sponsor of, and investors in, the hedge fund.

Under the changes introduced in the US under the Investment Advisers Act, hedge funds are now subject to many of the same requirements as retail funds, including registration with the SEC; designation of a Chief Compliance Officer; implementation of policies to prevent the misuse of non-public customer information, to ensure that client securities are voted in the best interests of the client; and implementation of a code of ethics. Hedge funds in the US were required to comply with all of these requirements by February 2006.

Fees

In most countries there are various laws and regulations that apply to the way in which the fund management company and managers, where the investment management is outsourced, are compensated for their work and services.

Basically this revolves around what the fund can be charged for and what the management company/manager absorb within any fee the fund itself pays to them.

Funds are usually required to have the fees and expenses disclosed in detail, as required by law, in a fee table included in every Prospectus or Scheme of Arrangement. They are presented in a standardised format, so that an investor can easily understand them and can compare expense ratios among different funds.

Hedge funds

There are no limits on the fees a hedge fund manager can charge its investors. Typically, the hedge fund manager charges an asset-based fee and a performance fee. Some have front-end or initial charges, as well.

Investment strategies and application

Most retail funds and trusts have restrictions that relate to gearing or borrowing powers against the value of securities in its portfolio. Many regulators require that funds engaging in certain investment techniques, including the use of options, futures, forward contracts and short-selling, "cover" their positions. The effect of these constraints has been to strictly limit the gearing or leveraging by retail funds in their portfolios.

However, with hedge funds, leveraging and other higher-risk investment strategies are common in hedge fund management. Hedge funds were originally designed to invest in equity securities and use leverage and short-selling to "hedge" the portfolio's exposure to movements of the equity markets. Today, however, advisers to hedge funds utilise a wide variety of investment strategies and techniques. Many are very active traders of securities creating, pro rata, far greater and more frequent changes to assets held in their portfolios and to the investment objectives and strategies.

Pricing and liquidity

By and large retail funds and authorised unit trusts are required to value their portfolios and price their securities daily based on market quotations that are readily available at market value and others at fair value, as determined in good faith by the board of directors. Also the fund/trust must be capable of providing investors with timely information regarding the value of their investments. Daily pricing is designed to ensure that both new investments and redemptions are made at accurate prices. Moreover, retail funds are required by law to allow shareholders to redeem their shares at any time.

As far as hedge funds are concerned there are no specific rules governing hedge fund pricing including the frequency of valuation of the portfolio. Hedge fund investors may be unable to determine the value of their investment at any given time although where a hedge fund is invested in by a retail fund or fund of hedge funds there will be a need for the hedge fund to value daily in order that the investing fund can accurately value their portfolio.

Types of investor

Mutual funds

The only qualification for investing in a retail fund or unit trust is having the minimum investment to open an account with the fund company or trust. After the account has been opened, there is generally no minimum additional investment required, and, whilst some investors invest a lump sum, many fund investors contribute relatively small amounts to their fund or unit trust on a regular basis as part of a long-term investment strategy.

Hedge funds

Investors must meet "qualifying status" and this can mean that a minimum investment of the equivalent of $1 million or more, or demonstration of significant wealth is often required of hedge fund investors.

The fund administrator/transfer agent is responsible for ensuring that an investor applying for shares in a hedge fund meets the regulatory requirement applicable to the fund.

Appendix 2

 THE COMMITTEE OF EUROPEAN SECURITIES REGULATORS

Ref: CESR/05-484

CESR's guidelines for supervisors regarding the notification procedure according to Section VIII of the UCITS Directive

Consultation Paper

October 2005

11-13 avenue de Friedland - 75008 PARIS - FRANCE - Tel.: 33.(0).1.58.36.43.21 - Fax: 33.(0).1.58.36.43.30
Web site: www.cesr-eu.org

Background

The 1985 UCITS Directive (85/611/EEC) introduced a passport for the investment funds harmonised by the Directive. The passport is based on mutual recognition. It foresees that the units of a UCITS authorised in its home Member State be marketed in other Member States subject only to a notification procedure set out in Art. 46 of the Directive.

The UCITS Directive requires the host authority to recognise the UCITS authorisation conferred by the home authorities. The notification procedure of Art. 46 does not encompass verification by the host authority of the extent to which the UCITS complies with the provisions governing authorisation as a UCITS. Section VIII of the UCITS Directive does however foresee residual powers for the host authority in verifying marketing arrangements for the UCITS and requires filing of a set of documents with the host authorities – in a language which is accepted by the host authority. The UCITS may begin to market its units two months after such filing unless the host authority issues a reasoned opinion regarding the inconsistency of the UCITS with those remaining provisions of host country laws, regulations and administrative provisions which may apply.

The UCITS passport is widely used. Over 29'000 cross-border notifications have been filed. Cross-border funds are competing successfully in many host country markets. However, the day-to-day operation of the notification procedure has in some instances been characterized by complication and uncertainty. These uncertainties also give rise to compliance cost and unnecessary delays.

These costs and delays are an important source of friction in a European market which has to date evolved without extensive fraud or mis-selling on a cross-border basis. It is therefore important, from a practical and legal perspective to do everything possible to facilitate the smoother functioning of the UCITS passport. This is why CESR members have decided that, following the work done regarding the transitional provisions of the UCITS III which has already contributed significantly to the notification process, the CESR Expert Group on Investment Management would conduct additional work on this area. The objective is to develop consistent standards for the notification requirements foreseen by the UCITS Directive. The importance of progress in this respect has been underlined by the Commission's Green Paper on investment funds last July.

This work takes place against the backdrop of two decades of divergent national practice in the enforcement of provisions of UCITS law – tolerated by ambiguities in the text of the Directive. Some of these differences are hard-coded in national law. In addition, there are areas of national law such as administrative law which influence the notification procedure but which are not subject to harmonization. These differences in national law hinder speedy alignment on a single approach to the notification procedure.

This work on notification procedures has to be seen in the context of the work CESR is currently undertaking on "eligible assets" of UCITS. Confidence that products notified for marketing are indeed UCITS-compliant is important to facilitate the stream-lined operation of notification requirements. The parallel work on clarification of 'eligible assets' is therefore important in achieving a fully functional European passport for UCITS.

<u>Purpose</u>

This document presents proposals for a common approach to the administration, by host authorities, of the notification procedures set out in Art. 46 of the Directive. The proposed arrangements seek to bring greater transparency and certainty to the notification process. The proposals aim to avoid uncertainty and prolongation of notification procedures. They do so, inter alia, by clarifying the way in which host authorities should communicate grounded and demonstrable concerns regarding the UCITS' compliance with any applicable host law under Art. 44(1) and Art. 45 of the Directive. The proposals also enshrine common approaches to the documentation that must be submitted in the context of the notification procedure and to clarify the handling of sub-funds of umbrella funds.

Some of the proposals for speedier processing cannot be guaranteed by all host authorities due to limitations imposed by national laws or regulations. However, there is a general commitment by all authorities to accelerate the processing of notifications where possible.

This consultation document from CESR seeks comments of all interested parties on the proposed guidelines on the notification procedure of UCITS. It is stressed that any proposal by CESR to simplify the notification procedure has to be in consistency with the provisions of the current UCITS Directive, including the competences given to host Member State authorities.

<u>Consultation Period</u>

The consultation closes on **27 January 2006**. Responses to the consultation should be sent via CESR's website (<u>www.cesr-eu.org</u>) under the section "Consultations".

INDEX

Introduction

Definitions

1. CESR invites responses to this consultation paper on its proposed guidelines on the notification procedure of UCITS. Respondents to this consultation paper can post their comments directly on CESR's website (www.cesr-eu.org) under the section "Consultations".

2. This document is aimed at receiving responses to its content and to the specific questions included in the document. CESR has included a number of questions to highlight those areas in which it would be particularly helpful to have the views of respondents. Comments are, of course, welcome on all aspects of the proposed CESR guidelines but, if changes are required, any reasoning accompanied by practical examples of the impact of the proposals will be very useful. CESR also welcomes specific drafting proposals when respondents are seeking changes to the proposed guidelines.

Background

3. The 1985 UCITS Directive (85/611/EEC) introduced a passport for the investment funds harmonised by the Directive. The passport is based on mutual recognition. It allows the units of a UCITS authorised in its home Member State to be marketed in other Member States without seeking authorisation in those host States, provided that the notification requirements of Art. 46 of the Directive are fulfilled. This provision was only slightly amended by the amending UCITS Directive 2001/107/EC, while requirements concerning a new management company passport were added to the Directive.

4. The Asset Management Expert Group reviewed last year for the European Commission the status of the European regulation on investment management. In its final report in May 2004 the requirement for an investment fund to be registered separately in each host Member State was regarded as a key barrier to efficient cross border fund distribution. The notification procedure has developed to be a de facto registration procedure, which can be very time consuming and may increase costs significantly for the UCITS and, ultimately, its investors. The requirements e.g. on which documents have to be presented differ from market to market. The Group considered that the current system should be replaced by a simple notification procedure. As a first step, the Group recommended that CESR in co-operation with the Commission should develop consistent standards for the registration requirements foreseen by the UCITS Directive to streamline the registration process.

5. The mandate approved by CESR to the CESR Expert Group on Investment Management (Ref: CESR/04-160) was published on 9th June 2004. According to the mandate, following the work done regarding the transitional provisions of the UCITS III, which would already affect significantly the notification process, the Expert Group would conduct additional work on this area to develop consistent standards for the notification requirements foreseen by the UCITS Directive to streamline the notification process. CESR's guidelines for the notification procedure have also been included in the list of priority actions in the Commission Green Paper on the enhancement of the EU framework for investment funds, published 14th July 2005.

6. CESR published a Call for Evidence on 9th June 2004 (Ref: CESR/04-267b) on the mandate inviting all interested parties to submit views as to what CESR should consider in its future work on investment management. CESR received 13 submissions and these can be viewed on

CESR's website. The simplification of notification requirements was considered as a priority issue by many respondents to the call for evidence. Standardisation and streamlining of processes was considered to provide a significant benefit to cross border distribution of UCITS. Furthermore, it was raised that attention should be paid to avoid the introduction of the management company passport and any ensuing registration duties annulling the efficiency gains that may be achieved in the fund registration area. CESR was asked to avoid the disparity of management company's registration requirements from arising/growing by agreeing, at this early stage, on standardised requirements and formats that are shared by all Member States.

Objective of the guidelines

7. CESR proposes to draft guidelines that will facilitate the consistency of practices regarding the notification procedure of UCITS. The aim of CESR is to develop operational guidelines which are easy to understand and to use, and which at the same time provide an efficient and adequate response for the protection of investors and for the development and the competitiveness of the single European investment fund market. The guidelines aim to promote convergence, certainty and transparency to the supervisory practises.

8. The main aims of these guidelines can be summarised as follows:

    -       Avoiding uncertainty related to procedures and necessary documents for a UCITS which <u>proposes to market</u> its units in a Member State other than that in which it is situated.

    -       Avoiding uncertainty related to procedures and necessary documents for a UCITS which <u>wants to maintain its authorisation for marketing</u> in a Member State other than that in which it is situated.

9. These guidelines are developed to harmonise the key points affecting the notification procedure, not all the related details, keeping in mind proportionality between procedures to be set up and objectives to be achieved.

10. The elaboration of the guidelines will not only facilitate a consistent approach to these supervisory issues across the EU but also ensure, by way of this prior public consultation, that the views from market participants and end-users will be fully considered.

11. The outcome of CESR's work will be reflected in common guidelines which do not constitute European Union legislation. CESR Members will introduce these guidelines in their day-to-day regulatory practices on a voluntary basis.

12. CESR's guidelines will not prejudice, in any case, the role of the Commission as guardian of the Treaties.

13. Preparation of these guidelines is being undertaken by the Expert Group on Investment Management. The Group is chaired by Mr Lamberto Cardia, Chairman of the Italian securities regulator, the Commissione nazionale per le società e la Borsa (CONSOB) and supported by Mr Jarkko Syyrilä from the CESR Secretariat. The Expert Group set up a working sub-group on this issue, coordinated by Mr Thomas Neumann of the German financial regulator, Bundesanstalt für Finanzdienstleistungsaufsicht (BaFin). The Expert Group is assisted by the Consultative Working Group on Investment Management composed of 16 market practitioners and consumers' representatives.

References

14. Documents already published by CESR which are relevant to this consultation paper are:

- *CESR starts work on its agenda for investment management (CESR/04-267b)*

- *Mandate for the Expert Group on Investment Management (CESR/04-160)*

- *CESR's guidelines for supervisors regarding the transitional provisions of the amending UCITS Directives (2001/107/EC and 2001/108/EC) (CESR/04-434b)*

CESR

DRAFT GUIDELINES

Definitions

1 References in this consultation paper to the "Directive" mean, unless the context requires otherwise, Directive 85/611/EEC of the Council of 20 December 1985 on the coordination of laws, regulations and administrative provisions relating to undertakings for collective investment in transferable securities (UCITS), as subsequently amended.

2 References in this consultation paper to terms defined in the Directive shall have the meaning given to them in the Directive.

General reservation

CESR Members are committed to act in accordance with these guidelines to simplify the notification procedure of UCITS. The draft guidelines contain various proposals on how to deal with issues related to the notification procedure in practice and how to facilitate a practicable application of the Directive.

However, as a consequence of the commitment of CESR Members to implement these guidelines, the amendment of their national legal provisions might be necessary. In many Member States this might also require a formal legislation procedure. Hence, in those cases a transitional period would be necessary for these CESR Members to implement the guidelines. This general reservation is without prejudice to Paragraph 11 of the Introduction.

A. Procedure

3   For marketing of units of a UCITS in other Member States than those in which the UCITS is situated, Section VIII of the UCITS Directive applies. If the UCITS proposes to market its units in a Member State other than that in which it is situated, it must first notify the competent authority of that other Member State in advance.

4   According to the UCITS Directive, the host Member State authority's competences are confined to refusing the marketing of a foreign UCITS on its territory in case the marketing arrangements do not comply with the provisions referred to in Art. 44(1) and Art. 45 of the Directive. CESR Members agree that other reasons, for instance those deriving from divergent interpretations on whether a UCITS complies with the Directive, can not be used as a reason to refuse the marketing according to the Directive. In other words, if the marketing arrangements comply with the provisions referred to in Art. 44(1) and Art. 45, the passport of the UCITS has to be respected.

5   The Directive does not provide for tools to deal with such type of problems. In particular, they cannot be dealt with within the notification procedure according to Art. 46. Therefore, other solutions might need to be found. In this context, the results to be worked out by the CESR Task Force on Mediation which is mandated to develop a proposal for a general CESR *mediation mechanism*, should be awaited. The objective of such a mediation mechanism is to facilitate a rapid, effective and balanced solution to disputes between home and host State authorities in order to facilitate convergence and the fair implementation and application of the Directive and these guidelines.

6   CESR suggests that for this notification procedure – as far as the harmonized part is concerned – a standardized notification letter is used by the UCITS. The draft model of the letter is attached to these guidelines (Annex II). This standardised European model for a notification letter as a part of the notification procedure will help to facilitate the notification procedure and provides the host State with a summary of the necessary information to process the notification.

7   The notification letter as well as all other documents and information required in the notification procedure as mentioned in these guidelines may also be submitted electronically, for example via fax or e-mail, if this is permitted by the law of the host State. As a best practice, CESR Members agree to facilitate electronic filing of documents, as far as it is possible taking into account the national legal framework and available IT-resources of CESR Members.

I. The two-month period

8   An investment company or a management company may begin to market the units of UCITS in the host Member State two months after it has completed the notification by submitting the required information and documents to the competent host State authority. This is however without prejudice to Art. 6a and Art. 6b of the Directive concerning the management company passport. CESR has so far dealt with the "product passport" procedure, which is clearly the most urgent concern for the markets. The management company passport has only been dealt with regarding the necessary information to be provided for the application of Art. 6b(5) in the attestation and the notification letter (Annexes I and II). As explained in footnote 1 of Annex I, providing the necessary

information regarding the management company in the "product notification" makes a separate
notification procedure regarding the management company unnecessary.

1. Starting the two-month period

9　The two-month period starts if the competent host State authority has received the complete
notification. If the notification is not complete, the two-month period does not start.

10　The notification is complete if all information and documents as provided for in the Directive and
these guidelines (cf. A.II., A.III., B. and D.) including its annexes (cf. E.) have been received by the
competent authority of the host Member State. The text of the documents may not have any
deletions in comparison with the documents which have been provided to the home Member State
authority except to the extent that the changes are prescribed in the Directive or in the applicable
provisions of the law of the host State. This circumstance will be attested by the UCITS in the
notification letter.

11　If the notification is incomplete, the competent host State authority shall inform the UCITS about
the incompleteness and the missing information and documents as soon as possible and in any case
within one month from the date of receipt of the notification letter.

12　Host States may provide in their national law that the missing documents and information must be
submitted by the UCITS upon request by the host Member State authority to this authority within a
defined time period after the request to amend the original notification material. This is done to
avoid a notification process to be held open for a long time period (e.g. one year) due to the UCITS
not providing the requested additional information. The aim of this requirement is to direct the
resources of authorities to applications that are still in the 'active phase'.

13　If provided for by national legislation or on a voluntary basis the host State can also confirm the
date of receipt of the complete notification within one month to inform the UCITS regarding the
date of the start of the two-month period (cf. D).

Q1:　Is the starting of the two-month period dealt with in a practicable way in your view?

---

2. Shortening the two-month period

14　The two-month period is the maximum period available for the host State competent authority to
check the notification.

15　The two-month period can be shortened. CESR Members agree that if permitted by the national law
of the host State, the competent authority can after checking the notification inform the UCITS that
it can start the marketing in the host State immediately, even if the two month-period is still going
on. CESR Members are committed to adopt on best efforts basis working procedures that will speed
up the notification process.

3. Managing the two-month period

16   Art. 46(2) of the Directive provides that a UCITS may start marketing its units two months after the communication of the required information and documents unless the host Member State authority establishes in *a reasoned decision* that the marketing arrangements do not comply with Art. 44(1) and Art. 45.

17   However, the Directive does not expressly explain the details of the reasoned decision. The procedures regarding the issuing of a reasoned decision are governed by national law. In fact the ways the Member States have implemented this provision have lead to uncertainties. CESR Members have therefore agreed on the following common approach regarding the use of the reasoned decision in practice.

18   The proposal aims at striking a balance between the needs of the host State authority for adequate information, and the desire of the UCITS to start marketing. The approach should therefore neither allow the UCITS to shorten the review period available to the host State authority by delaying the submission of necessary additional information, for instance by submitting it to the host authority at the very last moments of the two-month period, nor allow host Member States to unfairly delay the marketing of the UCITS.

19   As presented above, the competent authority of the host State has two months to check the contents of the notification, after it has received the complete notification. <u>During this two-month period the host State authority has to inform the UCITS, if in its view the submitted documents/ information imply that the marketing arrangements by the UCITS would not comply with Art. 44(1) and Art. 45 of the Directive.</u>

20   In the course of this two-month period the host State authority may solicit clarification of information from the UCITS regarding the elements under the residual competences of the host Member State according to Art. 44(1) and Art. 45 of the Directive. Such informal exchanges at the initiative of the host authority are without prejudice to the right of the UCITS to start marketing after the two-month period. In other words, unless a formal communication is provided to the UCITS by the competent host State authorities, it can start the marketing after the two-month period.

21   Based on practical experience CESR Members are sometimes confronted with the following situation: According to their check of the submitted documents the marketing arrangements by the UCITS would not comply with Art. 44(1) and Art. 45 of the Directive. This would justify the use of a reasoned decision.

22   In these cases where the authority can assume that there is a realistic prospect that compliance with Art. 44(1) and Art. 45 from the applicant's side can be achieved, the following more graduated approach should be applied.

23   The host Member State authority may inform the UCITS in a written procedure, via *a duly motivated communication,* that it considers that there are convincing arguments to believe that the requirements to make a reasoned decision preventing the UCITS to start marketing are fulfilled, unless the host State authority receives the necessary information it explicitly requires.

24 Taking into account that the UCITS has a commercial interest to start the marketing very quickly, it will normally provide the required information as soon as possible. After receiving the required information, the host State authority will finalise the checking of the notification in the remaining time that was left of the two-month period, when the host State authority required for the additional information. If the notification does still not fulfil the requirements of Art. 44(1) and Art. 45, the host State authority will formalise its reasoned decision in the remaining time of the two-month period, to prevent the UCITS from starting the marketing.

25 Applying this approach to the following example would mean:

- Receipt of the complete notification file by the host State authority: <u>7 July</u>

- Check on the compliance with Art. 44(1) and Art. 45 of the Directive of the notification and regular expiring of the two-month period: <u>7 September</u>

- Non-compliance with Art. 44(1) and Art. 45 communicated via a duly motivated communication by the host State authority to the UCITS: in this case <u>12 August</u> (i.e. remaining time until regular expiring of the two-month period on 7 September: <u>26 days</u>)

- Receipt of the requested information in the requested quality by the host State authority: in this case <u>26 August</u> (i.e. start of the remaining time of the two-month period of 26 days)

- Expiring of the two-month period: 26 August + 26 days = <u>21 September</u> (which is also equal to the regular expiring of the two-month period on 7 September + 14 days, i.e. the time it took the applicant to submit the requested information).

- The deadline is in any case without prejudice to the possibility of the host Member State authority to shorten the two-month period, if this is permitted by the national law of the host State.

Q2: Respondents are asked to provide their view on the practicability of the proposed approach.

II. Certification of documents

26 The latest versions of the necessary documents to be attached to the notification letter (cf. Annex II), as approved by or filed with[1] the home State authority, must be sent to the host State authority.

---

[1] The terms "approved by or filed with" the competent home State Authority are both used in this document because of the fact that in some Member States e.g. prospectuses of the UCITS and amendments thereto are approved by the competent authority, whereas in other Member States only the fund rules/ instruments of incorporation are approved, and prospectuses are only filed with the authority.

27 CESR has discussed different ways on how it could be given evidence that it is always the latest version of the documents which is sent to the host State authority, after an attestation pursuant to Art. 46 of the Directive has been issued by the home State authority. This discussion is especially of relevance for the modifications and on-going process (cf. C). Art. 4(4), 30 and 32 of the Directive provide that the fund rules may only be amended with the approval of the competent authorities and that the UCITS must send its simplified and full prospectuses and any amendments thereto keeping them up-to-date, to the competent authorities. On the other hand, according to Art. 46 of the Directive the host State authority is not entitled to a further quality check of the documents concerning their compliance with the Directive without prejudice to Art. 44(1) and Art. 45 of the Directive (cf. especially Annex I Schedule A, No 4 of the Directive) once the attestation pursuant to Art. 46 of the Directive was issued. In this situation it could happen that documents are sent to the host State authority which do not correspond to the documents sent by the UCITS to its home State authority to comply with Art. 4(4), 30 and 32 of the Directive. Thus, documents could be circulated to the investors in the host State which neither have been filed with or approved by the home or host State competent authority.

28 Currently many Member States require the certification of the documents related to the notification procedure for UCITS. This is done to make sure, that the documents provided to the host State authorities are the most recent ones approved by or filed with the home State authority.

29 To simplify the supervisory practice in this respect, CESR Members agree, that a host Member State authority may require such a certification of the simplified prospectus. CESR Members agree that such certification is not necessary for any other documents. The simplified prospectus is considered to be the most essential document regarding the fund for the investor, the key tool to make well-informed investment decisions, as regulated by the amended UCITS Directive. The simplified prospectus is indeed the key element of the marketing of the UCITS in the host State. Therefore the simplified prospectus and its proper translation can be relevant for the supervision of the marketing of UCITS which is under competence of the host State. It is very important that the host authorities can be sure which is the latest version of the simplified prospectus.

30 All host State authorities do not consider specific certification necessary, therefore the UCITS would need to provide the certified simplified prospectus only to the authorities of those Member States, that explicitly require it. To facilitate transparency of the requirements to the UCITS, these jurisdictions should indicate the requirement on their websites among the requirements on national marketing rules as stated in Annex III.

31 CESR Members agree that in case the simplified prospectuses of the UCITS are published on an official website in the internet under the responsibility of the home State authority, no further confirmation measures by the home State authority are needed, because the documents are in that case available also for the host State authorities when they need to know which are the latest versions of the documents.

32 CESR Members are committed to work in close cooperation when acting as home/ host Member State authorities, and to provide timely to the host authorities the necessary information that these might require in potential enforcement cases, to facilitate the proper functioning of the regulatory system in accordance with Art. 50(1) and Art. 52.

33   CESR has also discussed the possible benefits of the use of the Hague-Apostille as a means for certification of documents, and concluded that it is not necessary. <u>CESR Members therefore agree not to require the use of the Hague-Apostille for certification of documents.</u>

Q3:   Respondents are asked to provide their view on the practicability of the proposed approach.

III. Translation

34   The notification according to Art. 46 of the Directive including the documents which have to be submitted by the UCITS must be sent in the original language and translated into the or one of the official languages of the host State.

35   Since the documents are distributed to the investors, only a correct translation ensures that the information which has to be provided to the investors in the host Member State is actually transmitted to them. However, it is neither the task of the competent host State authority nor would it be possible to check whether the translations are consistent with the original versions. Therefore, the translated versions should be primarily literal translations of the latest original language versions approved by or filed with the home State authority. The translation has to be correct, i.e. the documents have to be understandable and should not contain material errors, omissions or misleading expressions. Supplementary text, modifications, omissions or any other changes to the text in the translated version are permissible only to the extent that the changes are prescribed by the Directive and by the applicable provisions of the law of the host Member State.

36   Correct, sufficient, and unambiguous information for the investor is one of the core elements of investor protection provided for by the Directive.

37   In accordance with Art. 47(2), the competent authorities of the host Member State can approve also the use of another language than the official language. To facilitate transparency of the language requirements to the UCITS, CESR Members will provide information on these requirements on their websites (cf. Annex III).

Q4:   Do you consider the suggested approach as appropriate?

IV. Umbrella funds

38   Though umbrella funds are acknowledged by the market practice and also the supervisory practice under the UCITS Directive, the Directive does not further address their treatment. However, CESR Members agree that in an umbrella UCITS all sub-funds must comply with the UCITS Directive. Nevertheless, sub-funds of an umbrella fund sometimes differ between themselves as regards the marketing arrangements in the host State (e.g. distribution channels).

39   Member States have developed different approaches on how to deal with the characteristics of umbrella funds with respect to the notification procedure.

1. Marketing of only part of the sub-funds

40   As stated in Art. 46 of the Directive, a UCITS has to inform the host State authority if it proposes to market its units in the host State. However, the Directive does not define the term "marketing" and how it could be interpreted especially for the application of Art. 46 of the Directive. Thus, from the Directive's perspective it is not clear when a UCITS or the sub-fund of an umbrella UCITS might be marketed in a Member State with the consequence that the host State authority has to be informed by a notification procedure before the start of marketing.

41   As a result, Member States have provided own definitions of marketing in their national law. The scope of marketing varies from a narrow understanding to a very broad understanding. Especially with regard to the full prospectus or other documents of the umbrella UCITS published and offered in the host State, including a description of all existing sub-funds, the offer to switch units between the different sub-funds and thereby the offer to sign units of every sub-fund, these activities are considered to be marketing of all sub-funds in those Member States where a broad definition of marketing prevails. As a consequence, those host States generally require a notification of each single sub-fund of the umbrella fund, even if the umbrella intends to market actively only a few sub-funds. This procedure would also apply when a new sub-fund is established under the umbrella although from the UCITS' perspective active marketing of this sub-fund is not intended in the host State. On the other side, where a narrower understanding of marketing prevails, other host State authorities only require the notification of those sub-funds which are actively marketed.

42   A harmonized definition of the terms "marketing" and "proposes to market" has not been dealt with so far in CESR's work, because the interpretation of these definitions is pending with the EU Commission. Until a common understanding has been formed, it is at national discretion how to define this criterion.

43   However, without prejudice to the general reservation of CESR Members as referred to under paragraph 2 of the draft guidelines, <u>CESR Members agree that if a UCITS intends to market actively only part of the sub-funds of an umbrella UCITS in the host State, only those sub-funds proposed to be marketed actively have to be notified.</u>

2. Notification procedure for new sub-funds

44   As outlined above, some Member States currently require the notification of the umbrella fund as a whole including a notification of all its sub-funds. Some other Member States just require those sub-funds that are actively marketed to be notified. If new sub-funds are added they request a separate notification procedure of the added sub-funds including the application of the two-month

period, which can be shortened if this is permitted by the national legislation. A third group of Member States requires the notification of the umbrella and the sub-funds to be actively marketed and consider the adding of further sub-funds as a modification of the notification of the umbrella. In this case, the documents for the respective sub-fund including the marketing arrangements have to be filed but the two-month period is not applied.

45   For simplification purposes CESR Members agree on the following:

1) Instead of a separate notification of each sub-fund it is possible to include all sub-funds in one notification letter if these notices are provided simultaneously. Furthermore, cross-references concerning documents, for instance if the articles of incorporation of the overall umbrella have remained unchanged can be made and therefore the documents have only to be submitted once.

2) If in a later stage the UCITS intends to market sub-funds, which were already included in the original notification material, but which were not proposed to be marketed in the host State at that stage (cf. Paragraph 43), without changing the marketing arrangements already in place for other sub-funds, and to the extent that the relevant information already submitted is unchanged, a simple communication concerning the adding of these sub-funds is needed and the two-month period does not apply. The adoption of this practise is an option that the host State authority may use, if it considers this might provide additional flexibility in the notification process. CESR Members will inform on their websites, if they adopt this practice (cf. Annex III).

3) If new sub-funds are added to the umbrella fund and these sub-funds are proposed to be marketed in the host State, the notification procedure and the two-month period applies; this procedure also applies in case the above option no. 2) is not made use of in the host State. This is in order to allow the host State authority to examine e.g. the translation of the prospectus. The two-month period may be shortened if this is permitted by the national legislation of the host State.

All host authorities do not consider it necessary to apply the two-month period in the latter case. To facilitate transparency of the requirements to the UCITS, the jurisdictions that will apply the two-month period should indicate the requirement on their websites among the requirements on national marketing rules as stated in Annex III.

Q5: Do you consider the suggested approach as appropriate?

B. Content of the file

46   UCITS should not be obliged by the host State to send other documents and information than those mentioned in this chapter, however without prejudice to the documents and information due to Art. 44(1) and Art. 45 of the Directive. This chapter only deals with the documents and information required according to Art. 46 of the Directive whilst the documents and information due to Art. 44(1) and Art. 45 of the Directive are dealt with in Chapters D. and in Annex III and Annex IV.

47 If a UCITS proposes to market its units in a host State, it must first inform the competent host State authority of its intention and provide the following documents and information:

1. a valid original attestation granted by the competent home Member State authority, to the effect that the UCITS fulfils the conditions imposed by the Directive (cf. Annex I, with a model attestation to market units of UCITS in an EEA Member State);

2. a notification letter (cf. Annex II, with a model notification letter to market units of UCITS in an EEA Member State);

3. its latest up-to-date fund rules or instruments of incorporation (they need not be submitted separately if they are included in the prospectus; the latter must be indicated by the notifying UCITS or a third person empowered by written mandate to act on behalf of the notifying UCITS);

4. its latest up-to-date full and simplified prospectuses, containing all information as provided for by Art. 28(2) including Schedule A of Annex I and Art. 28(3) including Schedule C of Annex I of the Directive, and as endorsed by the Commission's Recommendation on some contents of the simplified prospectus[1];

5. its latest published annual report and any subsequent half-yearly report; and

6. details of the arrangements made for the marketing of units in the host Member State (cf. Annexes III and IV).

Q6: Do you consider the suggested approach as appropriate?

C. Modifications and on-going process

48 Generally according to Art. 47 of the Directive, documents and information have to be published in the host State in accordance with the same procedures as those provided for in the home State. In CESR Members' view it is important that the investors in the host State have the same information available as the investors in the home State.

49 Based on the reference of Art. 47 to Art. 29 and Art. 30 of the Directive, Member States expect foreign UCITS to keep their documents and information up-to-date, e.g. any amendments to the fund rules or instruments of incorporation (which do not need to be submitted separately if they are included in the full prospectus; the latter must be certified by the notifying UCITS or a third

---

[1] Commission Recommendation 2004/384/EC of 27 April 2004 on some contents of the simplified prospectus as provided for in Schedule C of Annex I to Council Directive 85/611/EEC, OJ L 144, 30.4.2004, p. 42.

person empowered by written mandate to act on behalf of the notifying UCITS), the full and/or simplified prospectuses, or new prospectuses, if applicable, have to be sent to the competent authority in the host State; also the latest published annual report and any subsequent half-yearly report have to be submitted.

50   The guidelines set out in chapters A.II., III. and B, where applicable, also apply if a UCITS notifies the host State authority of any modifications of the fund rules or instruments of incorporation, the full and/or simplified prospectuses, or, if applicable, the introduction of new prospectuses.

Q7:   Do you consider the suggested approach as appropriate?

D. National marketing rules and other specific national regulations

51   This chapter deals with the non-harmonized national provisions which relate to the application of the Directive. Non-harmonized provisions may be found in each Member State, as the Directive either expressly does not rule on a specific issue in detail and instead instructs the Member States to deal with the particulars of this issue in their own national legislation, or the Directive is simply silent regarding an issue and thus leaves room for interpretation of this issue by national law of each Member State. Thus, the same issue may be either subject to diverging regulations in Member States, or an issue may be subject to regulation in a jurisdiction whilst it is not regulated in the national law of another Member State.

52   Due to Art. 45 of the Directive, UCITS are obliged to make facilities in the host State available for making payments to unit-holders, re-purchasing or redeeming units (e.g. paying agent) and for making available the information which UCITS are obliged to provide (e.g. information agent). The Directive does not rule these requirements in more detail and leaves it to the Member States how to establish and to design the respective facilities in their own national law.

53   According to Art. 44(2) of the Directive, UCITS must comply with the provisions governing advertising in the host State. Pursuant to Art. 44(1) of the Directive, UCITS which market their units in other Member States are required to comply also with the laws, regulations and administrative provisions in force in the host State which do not fall within the field governed by the Directive. This circumstance can also affect the notification procedure (for instance administrative law). Due to these legal provisions which are not harmonised, UCITS may also be required to fulfill certain requirements or may be required to send additional documents or information, other than those mentioned in Art. 46 of the Directive and listed in Chapter B. of these guidelines, to the host State authority.

54   According to these guidelines apart from Art. 44 and Art. 45 of the Directive the following issues are governed by national law:

– electronic submission of documents for example via fax or e-mail (cf. A. Procedure);

– confirmation of the date of receipt of the complete notification within one month to inform the UCITS of the date of the start of the two-month period (cf. A.I.1.);

– submission period for missing documents and information (cf. A.I.1.);

– shortening of the two-month period (cf. A.I.2.);

– submission of certified documents (cf. A.II.);

– marketing within the sense of Art. 46 of the Directive (cf. A.IV.1.); and

– transitional provisions with respect to the General reservation under point 2.

55 <u>To simplify the access to information for UCITS, the host State authorities will be requested to fill in Annex III of these guidelines and to publish it on their websites.</u> This Annex gives a standardized overview on the non-harmonized national provisions of a host State which relate to the application of the Directive. CESR Members are also expected to publish any amendment or abolition of these provisions or the enactment of new provisions to keep the compilation published with Annex III on their website up-to-date. Annex IV gives the details on which website each host State authority publishes its overview and where it can be downloaded. CESR Members are expected to inform CESR on any amendment of the internet address so that the Annex IV can be updated accordingly.

Q8: Do you agree with the proposals concerning the publication of the information or do you prefer another procedure and if, which one?

Q9: Do you feel that an issue in this consultation paper should be dealt with in more detail or that other aspects of an issue already contained in the consultation paper should also have been treated?

Q10: Should some additional issues related to the notification procedure have been dealt with in this consultation paper, and if yes, which?

ANNEXES TO THE CONSULTATION PAPER

Annex I

MODEL ATTESTATION TO MARKET UNITS OF UCITS IN AN EEA MEMBER STATE

1   ……………...…..……………………………………………………… is the competent authority
(name of the competent home Member State authority)

2   in ………………………………………………………………………………………………………..
(the home Member State)

3   *address* ………………………………………………………………………………….…………………

4   *telephone number* ……………………………………………………...……………………………………

5   *telefax number* ……………………………………………………………………………………………

6   *e-mail address* ……………………………………………………………………………………………

7   that carries out the duties provided for in the Directive 85/611/EEC on the coordination of laws, regulations and administrative provisions relating to undertakings for collective investment in transferable securities (UCITS) (hereinafter, the Directive), as required by Art. 49(1) of the Directive.

8   For   the   purpose   of   Art.   46(1)   and   Art.   6b(5)[1]   of   the   Directive, ………...…..……………………………....………………………………………………………
(the competent home Member State authority)

9   certifies that:

……………………………………………………......……………………………………………,
(the name of the UCITS, i.e. the name of the common fund/ unit trust/ investment company)

10   - has been set up on ……………………………………………………………………………..,
(date of establishment of the UCITS)

---

[1] According to CESR's guidelines for supervisors regarding the transitional provisions of the amending UCITS Directives (Ref. CESR/04-434b), point B.I.2, "only a product passport and no management company passport shall be required if a management company only wishes to distribute UCITS managed by itself in a host Member State… All the information foreseen for notification of the management company is considered to be fully encompassed in the registration procedure for the product. This requires full confidence that the arrangements put in place effectively ensure compliance of the management company with the UCITS Directive (subject to the transitional arrangements … mentioned)." This guideline covers the marketing of funds via a third party. Even if CESR has not yet addressed more specifically issues concerning the management company notification procedure, the requirement of a UCITS-compliant management company with respect to Art. 6b(5) needs to be taken into account in any case within the product passport mechanism. Therefore it is suggested that the model attestation should include an element on the UCITS-compliance of the management company.

CESR

11   - has registry no. ....,
                    (UCITS' registry no. in the home Member State, if any)

       name of the authority ....,
                    (name of the authority by which the register is conducted, if applicable)

12   - is based in ....,
                    (the home Member State and details of the address of the UCITS' head office)

13   - is   ☐ a common fund/unit trust,

List of sub-funds to be marketed in the host Member State, if applicable	
Serial no.	Name
1	
2	
3	
...	

                    ▪   managed by the management company

                    ....
                                (name of the management company)

14
                    ☐   an investment company,

List of sub-funds to be marketed in the host Member State, if applicable	
Serial no.	Name
1	
2	
3	
...	

                    ▪   that has designated as its management company

                    ....
                                (name of the designated management company)

                    ▪   that is self-managed

15 - is   ☐ a grandfathered UCITS I, i.e. it is fully compliant with the requirements laid down in
             the Directive 85/611/EEC prior to its amendments by the Directive 2001/108/EC

16 - is   ☐ a UCITS III, i.e. it is fully compliant with the requirements laid down in the Directive
             85/611/EEC as amended by the Directive 2001/108/EC

17   ....….….……………………………………………………....………… also certifies that:
(the home Member State authority)

18   a) ……………………………………………………………………………………………
(name of the UCITS' management company, if applicable, according to what has been indicated above)

19   - is   ☐ a grandfathered UCITS I management company, i.e. it is fully compliant with the requirements laid down in the Directive 85/611/EEC prior to its amendments by the Directive 2001/107/EC

20   - is   ☐ a UCITS III management company, i.e. it is fully compliant with the requirements in the Directive 85/611/EEC as amended by the Directive 2001/107/EC

21   b) the latest version of the fund rules/instruments of incorporation has been approved by the home Member State competent authority on …………………… *(date of approval);*

22   Date ....

.... *(signature of the representative of the home Member State authority)*

.... *(name in full and position of the undersigned representative of the home Member State authority)*

Q11:   Is the model attestation practicable in your view?

Annex II

MODEL NOTIFICATION LETTER TO MARKET UNITS OF UCITS IN AN EEA MEMBER STATE

COMMUNICATION FOR MARKETING UCITS IN ....
(the host Member State)

PART A Harmonized part

1   Name of the UCITS:

....

2   Home Member State of the UCITS:

....

3   Legal form of the UCITS: *common fund/ unit trust/ investment company* (*please circle the correct choice*)

4   Does the UCITS have sub-funds or compartments: *yes/ no*

5   Name of the fund(s) and/or the   Duration (if applicable)   Code numbers in the
    sub-fund(s) to be marketed in   host MS, if available
    the host MS[1]   (e.g. ISIN-code):

....

....

....

....

....

....

....

....

---

[1] If the UCITS intends to market only some share classes it may list only these share classes.

6

> Management company/ Self-managed investment company:
>
> ....
>
> Address and registered office/seat/domicile if address and registered office/seat/domicile are not identical:
>
> ....
>
> Name, telephone number, telefax number and e-mail address of the contact person:
>
> ....
>
> Duration of the company, if applicable:
>
> ....
>
> Scope of activities of the management company in the host Member State:
>
> ....
> ....

7

> Possible additional comments of the UCITS:
>
> ....
> ....
> ....
> ....

Attached documents[1]:

8 __ A valid original attestation granted by the competent home Member State authority

9 __ The latest up-to-date fund rules or instruments of incorporation (they need not be submitted separately if they are included in the prospectus; the latter must be indicated by the notifying UCITS or a third person empowered by written mandate to act on behalf of the notifying UCITS).

10 __ The latest up-to-date full and simplified prospectus

11 __ The latest published annual report and any subsequent half-yearly report

---

[1] All documents must be sent in the original language and translated into at least one of the official languages of the host State, as explained in Chapter A.III.

12   *Note:* The notification letter may refer to documents that have already been sent to the host Member State competent authority, if still valid. The attestation from the home Member State competent authority must be sent in any case.

       PART B   Documents and information according to national marketing rules and other specific national regulations

13   __ Details of the arrangements made for the marketing of the units in the host Member State (cf. Annexes III and IV)

       Confirmation by the UCITS

14   I hereby confirm that the documents attached to this notification letter contain all relevant information as provided for in the Directive and CESR's guidelines regarding the notification procedure, including its annexes. The text of the documents does not have any deletions in comparison with the documents which have been provided to the home Member State authority but without prejudice to Art. 44(1) and Art. 45 of the Directive (cf. A.II. and especially Schedule A, Annex I, No. 4 of the Directive for full prospectus).

15   Date and place ....

             .... (signature of the authorised signatory of the UCITS or of a third person empowered by written mandate to act on behalf of the notifying UCITS)

             .... (name in full and position of the undersigned authorised signatory of the UCITS or of the third person empowered by written mandate to act on behalf of the notifying UCITS)

16   Explanatory text

       The model notification letter is the common model developed to cover the harmonised contents of the notification procedure according to Art. 46 and Art. 6b(5) of the Directive (see footnote 1 of the model attestation). However, in addition to this, there are national requirements regarding marketing arrangements and advertising based on Art. 44 and art. 45, which grant powers for host Member State competent authorities (the national provisions of the host country may include requirements concerning paying agents, representatives in the host Member State etc.). This means that in addition to the model notification letter, there would in practise be a national annex for each jurisdiction regarding the requirements that are in the national discretion of the host MS. To simplify the access to information, CESR Members will publish on their websites a standardized overview on the non-harmonized national provisions of a host State which relate to the application of the Directive. CESR Members are also expected to publish any amendment or abolition of these provisions or the enactment of new provisions to keep the compilation up-to-date.

       Q12:   Is the model notification letter practicable in your view?

Annex III

National marketing rules and other specific national regulations

I.   Member State

II.   Date of last update

III.   Supporting documents or information to the notification letter that are not required by the Directive but by national law (e.g. information in the full prospectus, certifications and/or written mandate, paying agent, information agent, other information, certifications of documents)

IV.   Additional information

    1.   electronic submission of documents for example via fax or e-mail: yes / no

    2.   two-month period may be shortened: yes / no

    3.   date of receipt of the complete notification is confirmed within one month: yes / no

    4.   maximum submission period for missing documents and information, if the notification is incomplete: yes / no

V.   Required languages for translation

VI.   Transitional provisions with respect to the General reservation under point 2

VII.   Documented evidence of fee payment

VII.   Conditions for ending marketing/ registration

VIII.   Other issues

Q13:   What would you suggest CESR to do regarding the national requirements to simplify the notification procedure?

Annex IV

List of CESR Members' websites for the downloading of national marketing rules and other national regulations regarding the notification process

[only presented as examples at this stage]

1. Germany

www.bafin.de | Für Anbieter | Investmentfonds | ausländische Investmentfonds

or

www.bafin.de/cgi-bin/bafin.pl?verz=0407010000&sprache=0&filter=&ntick=0

2. UK

www.fsa.gov.uk/pubs/other/cispr_02_eea.pdf

Annex V   Indicative CESR work plan on the guidelines on the notification procedure of UCITS

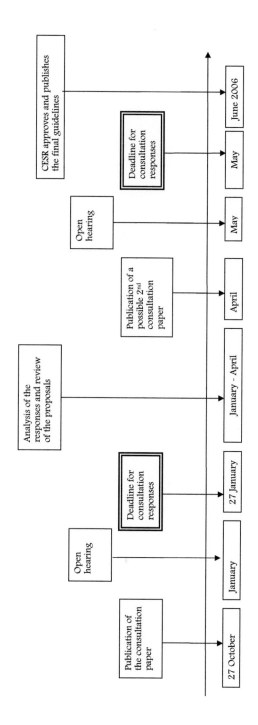

Index

Printed and bound by CPI Group (UK) Ltd, Croydon, CR0 4YY

08/05/2025

01864778-0001